ELVIS
IS
ALIVE

THE COMPLETE CONSPIRACY

XAVIANT HAZE

Adventures Unlimited Press

Elvis is Alive

by Xaviant Haze

Copyright © 2015

ISBN 978-1-939149-39-8

Published by:
Adventures Unlimited Press
One Adventure Place
Kempton, Illinois 60946 USA
auphq@frontiernet.net

www.AdventuresUnlimitedPress.com

ELVIS
IS
ALIVE

THE COMPLETE CONSPIRACY

XAVIANT HAZE

Adventures Unlimited Press

Elvis Presley

TABLE OF CONTENTS

This Book is dedicated to Sam

We will walk again old buddy, we will walk again....

ELVIS
IS
ALIVE

THE COMPLETE CONSPIRACY

XAVIANT HAZE

DAILY Mirror

BRITAIN'S BIGGEST DAILY SALE   7p   Wednesday, August 17, 1977

ELVIS PRESLEY IS DEAD

THE IDOL: Pop king Elvis Presley as his millions of fans throughout the world knew him.

ELVIS PRESLEY, the unchallenged king of Rock n' Roll, is dead.

And the 42-year-old superstar who had millions of adoring fans throughout the world, was alone when he died.

He died yesterday...

From **ANTHONY DELANO** in New York

THE ROCK WORLD MOURNS..

By JACK LEWIS

Heath

HUSBAND: Elvis with wife Priscilla, during their six-year marriage.

THE KING IS DEAD —See Centre Pages

INTRODUCTION

Oh Elvis, where art thou? For more than 35 years Elvis lovers have been asking themselves this question, desperately wanting to believe their musical hero is still alive. Most "conspiracy theories" begin to form immediately following an event, and it appears that the 'Elvis is alive' theory sprang up upon the announcement of the star's death. The 'Elvis is still alive' mindset has even become ingrained in the zeitgeist of pop culture, where no matter the generation, everyone has heard the crazy tales of Elvis being spotted coming out of a UFO, a KFC in Michigan or even living anonymously down in the Bayou. There is no denying that Elvis was the greatest performer that ever lived. His onstage charisma and ability to control the audience are unmatched. Even when Elvis was stoned out of his mind he still had the crowd in the palm of his hand. This astonishing stage presence, along with his incredible singing voice, made up for the fact that Elvis never wrote a song in his entire life despite recording more than 600 songs throughout his career.

Thanks to the advent of television, Elvis was the first superstar that teenage girls went absolute crazy for, and because of his sex appeal and youth, Elvis helped pushed rock 'n' roll into the mainstream—an art form that prior to the King's influence was only to be found in Southern black neighborhoods, concocted in mashed up blues experiments. Being a poor boy from the Deep South, Elvis was exposed to this music at an early age. His singing style and unique swiveling hips were all his, proving that Elvis was a self-made man albeit under the control of ruthless handlers cashing in on the white boy with that "Negro sound" to the tune of millions.

While his career was taking off, Elvis was forced into

the Army, where he stunned the high command by refusing to perform for the troops in USO tours and enlisted as just a regular grunt. It was during this spell in the Army that Elvis was introduced to amphetamine pills and it's also when his mother died, two events that mentally challenged him for the rest of his life. His mother's death also made it easier to manipulate Elvis, now emotionally susceptible to Monarch Butterfly Mind Control methods. Plus he came along exactly at the moment when the most powerful tool ever created for mind control was now in most every American home—the television.

After being discharged from the Army, Elvis was given a huge welcome home bash by Frank Sinatra at the Fontainebleau in Miami Beach. The special was broadcast on CBS and was a smashing success, garnering the highest ratings up to that point in the history of television. Elvis was then put through the wringer in Hollywood, and forced to "act" in countless crappy movies the studios turned out for huge profits. Elvis would inevitably set the bar for all other future superstars to be modeled after. Lost to the world and even himself would be the real Elvis, because whether it was on stage, in the movies or the recording studio, the name Elvis Presley meant big dollars. But later in his career when the film offers dried up, and the live shows were the butt of fat jokes, the Presley Empire was run into the ground thanks to an overdemanding tour schedule.

Poor Elvis had grown sick of it all; he couldn't go out in public without being recognized, and this torment forced him to experiment with various wigs and beards and hire a stream of body doubles to confuse the paparazzi. For all intents and purposes, Elvis was dying not to be Elvis anymore. He had grown depressed and fat, his fans and the media made fun of his karate-chopping antics and over-the-top diet. Needless to say, the King was exhausted with having to live up to the public's image of him and bored with being a prisoner. He also had an epic drug problem, and loved prescription pills so much he kept an encyclopedia of all the various pills and what effects they were good for handy at all times. This infamous pill addiction helped lead the King to an early "death." In the wake, a pop culture phenomenon was born, and Elvis has enjoyed a famous afterlife thanks to over three decades of conspiracy theories claiming he's still alive. It's time to reexamine these theories and put to rest once and for all the notion that Elvis could have faked his own death. If we can…

1.

THE MAN AND THE MYTH

Southern man
better keep your head
Don't forget
what your good book said
Southern change
gonna come at last
Now your crosses
are burning fast
Southern man
I saw cotton
and I saw black
Tall white mansions
and little shacks.
Southern man
when will you
pay them back?

— Neil Young

"When my father and my mother forsake me, then the LORD will take me up." — Psalms 27:10

"I never expected to be anybody important."— Elvis

The strange saga of Elvis Presley rising from dirt poor country singer to pop icon was a combination of hard work, luck, timing and the mysterious workings of the universe. The question of whether or not Elvis is alive is an afterthought; the real question is who was *he*? The epic Elvis family tree has roots in 16th century Germany. The family founder in America, Johannes Valentin Bressler, was born in the village of Hochstadt (where the Preslar family was first mentioned in 1494) in the Palatinate region of Germany. Bressler worked as a vine dresser before marrying Anna

13

Christiana Franse and emigrating to New York in 1710. By the 1800s the German surname Bressler became Presler, and finally Presley as decades passed. In 1727, the Presleys moved from New York through Pennsylvania to Maryland and then to Anson County, North Carolina where the clan continued to expand during the American Revolutionary War period.

After fighting in and surviving the war for independence, John Presley the great-grandson of the first Presley immigrant to American, relocated his family to Monroe County, Tennessee. The Civil War years took their toll on the Presley clan but they continued to scrape by on the fat of the land. By the early 1900s Elvis' grandfather Jessie Presley (the great-grandson of John) had drifted from sharecropping and lumberjack jobs throughout Mississippi, Kentucky, and Missouri before joining the Army to fight in World War I. On July 20, 1913 Jessie married Minnie Mae Hood and three years later Vernon Presley was born. But Elvis' father wasn't blessed with a good family upbringing as Jessie was almost always absent from his son's life. When Jessie was around, Vernon lived in fear of getting beaten up by his drunk old man. Jessie took off for good in 1945 leaving Minnie Mae and Vernon to fend for themselves in Tupelo, Mississippi. Elvis' grandma Minnie lived in the Graceland Mansion until her death in 1980.

Elvis' maternal heritage on his mother Gladys' side is even more interesting. His great-great-great-grandmother, Morning White Dove, was a full-blooded Cherokee Indian. This is likely where his high cheekbones and unique look come from. This might be the source of Elvis's spiritual and cognitive abilities, as well. Morning White Dove's husband, William Mansell, was of French lineage. The Mansells wandered from Normandy, France to Scotland, and then later to Ireland before coming to the American Colonies in the 18th century. The title "white" in Morning Dove's name refers to her status as a peaceful Indian, as opposed to a dangerous "red" Indian. Early American settlers commonly married "white" Indians due to the scarcity of women during the pioneering of the American frontier. William Mansell was a grizzled war veteran who fought with Andrew Jackson at the Battle of Horseshoe Bend during the Indian Wars of the early nineteenth century. Once the fighting ended he relocated his new family to Alabama and settled near the Mississippi border where the soil was fertile. Mansell built a house that sheltered their three offspring, the eldest of whom, John Mansell, born in 1828, happened to be Elvis' great-great-grandfather.

The Mansell family farm would be lost by the time of the Civil War and Elvis' great-grandfather, a hardworking sharecropper, barely survived the war's devastating aftermath. White married Martha Tackett on January 22, 1870 in Saltillo, Mississippi. Martha's mother, Nancy, practiced the Jewish religion, which was a rare thing to do in Mississippi during this time. Born in 1876, Doll Mansell, Gladys Presley's mother and Elvis' grandmother, the slim, porcelain-featured, spoiled third daughter of White Mansell was the apple of her father's eye. She did not marry until she was 27, and then to her first cousin, Robert Smith.

Elvis Presley's maternal grandparents were first cousins, a common occurrence in isolated communities in the South. Doll was usually bedridden from tuberculosis throughout the marriage, while Robert labored away as a sharecropper, barely able to support his sick wife and eight children. Elvis' mother, Gladys Smith, was born on April 25, 1912 with the noose of poverty around her neck. When she was the tender age of 19, her father unexpectedly died, which was a complete shock as everyone expected the sickly Doll to die first. Gladys didn't have a good relationship with her mother, and basically ran off with the first man who swept her off her feet, a 17-year-old Vernon Presley, four years her junior. Coincidentally Vernon didn't get along with his father, two intangibles the new lovebirds now shared, coupled with a long line of family poverty. Vernon and his brother Vester struggled to find work during the Depression, and took any job that came along, even attempting farming by raising soybeans and hogs. After this venture failed, Vernon drove delivery trucks for McCarty's, a Tupelo grocery store, for a number of years throughout northeast Mississippi. By

15

the end of June 1934, Vernon was back to working odd jobs while Gladys became pregnant.

By her fifth month she was bigger than normal and certain to be carrying twins. Vernon began working on Orville S. Bean's dairy farm and was able to borrow $180 from Bean to build a home for his family. With help from his father and brother, Vernon built a two-room shotgun shack with no electricity or indoor plumbing in East Tupelo, Mississippi, then known as the "roughest town in North Mississippi." The shack was located along Old Saltillo Road over a highway that ran locals to Birmingham. Elvis Presley was born here on January 8, 1935, during the midst of the Great Depression. Strangely enough his birth was presided over by an unidentified blue light that hovered in the sky over the home where Elvis was born. This blue light was reported by both Presley's father Vernon, and the doctor who delivered baby Elvis. According to Vernon Presley, he saw the UFO and blue light around two in the morning when he stepped outside to smoke a cigarette. [1]

But Elvis wasn't the only baby delivered on that fateful day; his twin Jesse Garon, failed to survive, making Elvis a "twin-less twin," a psychosomatic event that plagued Elvis his entire life. Psychologists have since proved that the loss of a twin has a lifelong effect on both the mother and surviving twin. Famous science fiction writer Philip K. Dick also suffered from the effects of being a twin-less twin, an unhealthy mental obsession that he shared with Elvis. The "phantom twin" theme occurred in a number of his works and his third wife Anne claimed that Dick believed that somehow he carried the soul of his dead twin sister inside him.

Elvis longed for his brother as he grew older and even had imaginary conversations with Jesse, claiming to have seen his ghost a few times. So obsessed was Elvis that he diligently changed his middle name, Aaron, to Aron, to match his twin's middle name Garon better. Elvis' mother planted an early seed in his head that a surviving twin inherits the strength of both children, and all

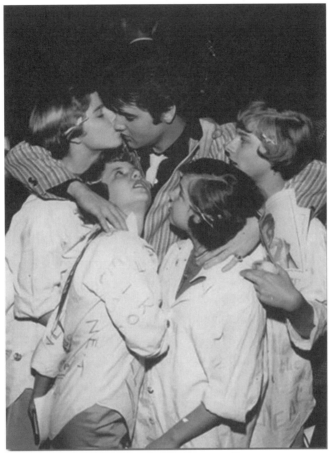

Elvis with adoring girls—AFP/Getty

evidence indicates that, in this case anyway, she was spot on. Elvis' hairdresser and spiritual advisor Larry Geller writes:

> The life and death of his stillborn twin brother, Jesse Garon, was a precious mystery to Elvis, an indelible part of his life. But then, Elvis was always intrigued by the mystery that lay at the heart of all existence. When it came to Jesse Garon, he told me that as a child he would talk about him to anyone who would listen. "I have a brother!" he announced proudly, telling everyone how close they were, and how they talked together all the time. At night as he lay in his bed, in the dark and silence of his room, he would have special conversations with Jesse, and later

tell people what his brother had said to him. I knew Elvis had a stillborn twin brother; my own younger twin sisters had told me after they read a story about him in a movie magazine. It was only after we met in April of 1964, that I came to realize how deeply Elvis had been affected by this unfulfilled relationship. "I'll tell ya Larry, being a twin has always been a mystery for me. I mean, we were in our mother's womb together, so why was he born dead and not me? He never even got his chance to live. Think about it, why me? Why was I the one that was chosen? An' I've always wondered what would've been if he had lived, I really have. These kinds of questions tear my head up. There's got to be reasons for all this."

This was our very first conversation. I was a virtual stranger, yet for some reason Elvis felt that he wanted to bare his soul about Jesse Garon. I learned over the years that this was one aspect of his life he rarely if ever spoke about. But on this particular afternoon he opened the floodgates freely, revealing something so intimate that it was obvious that he was deeply burdened by the notion that he might have survived at the expense of his twin. It wasn't until 1977, just a few months before Elvis' death that I heard him bring up Jesse after all those years. Elvis was so open; he loved to talk about anything under the sun. From sex, politics or religion, to intimate details about family, friends, wives, girlfriends, co-workers and private thoughts and feelings about his career and his own life, nothing was out of bounds. But I can't remember his ever really talking about Jesse Garon...not until one day in the spring while we were on tour. I entered his room while he was still in bed. "Lawrence," Elvis declared excitedly, "You won't believe the dream I just had. Man, it was so real. An' I can't remember dreaming about my brother Jesse Garon since I was a little kid. But there we were together—on stage. Seemed like thousands of people in the audience, and they were screaming at us.

It was wild! We were dressed alike, wearing identical white jumpsuits, and we were both playing matching guitars slung around our shoulders. There were two blue spotlights, one shining on him, one on me. An' I kept looking at him, and man, he was the spitting image of me. I'll tell you something else Lawrence..." Elvis grinned. "Jesse had a way better voice than me." [2]

The little shotgun shack child Elvis called home was lost when Vernon was sent to Parchman Farm—the Mississippi State Penitentiary—for eight months for altering a four-dollar check.

Childhood Church in Tupelo (Kevin King)

Three-year-old Elvis and his mother moved in with relatives until Vernon's release; thereafter the Presleys moved from one affordable place to another. The one constant in their lives was church, and the music booming from within this place of worship had an immediate effect on little Elvis.

By the time he was four, his psychic abilities were keen as he proclaimed that he was going to buy his mother and father each a Cadillac. He announced this during an argument they were having

Inside the Church (Kevin King)

over money and paying the bills. Elvis' uncanny gift of psychic understanding continued throughout his life. His mother Gladys also possessed this rare trait. One famous example was a dream she had of Elvis in a burning car; Elvis and Red West did have this psychic event happen to them but escaped in time to avoid any serious damage. Red recalls Mrs. Presley's uncontrollable clairvoyance:

Birthplace of Elvis (Ken Lund)

There was always something eerie about the things she would say. Like she was a psychic or something like it. Whenever we had a particular wild scene on stage or if a riot broke out, whenever Elvis called her she would somehow have some premonition that someone got out of hand even before reading the newspapers...I tell you this because it always struck me as if there was something really strange about the Presley's. All this sleepwalking and dreaming were all somehow related to some kind of special powers I don't really understand or could put my finger on. A lot of the psychic stuff is bunk, but to some degree I believe in it. Elvis proved it to me again and again.[3]

At age ten Elvis was going to elementary school, taking guitar lessons and reading comic books like Captain Marvel Jr.; in just a few years he would be bringing Captain Marvel's hairstyle and flashy outfits into trailblazing fashion. Impressed with his musical abilities, Oleta Grimes, one of his teachers, entered Elvis in a talent contest at the Mississippi-Alabama Fair. He sang "Old Shep" before several hundred people and his stunned mother, and won fifth place for his first-ever public performance. A year later Elvis' parents spent $12.95 at the Tupelo Hardware Company, buying him his first guitar.

He began taking the guitar with him everywhere he went and even played a little gospel music sometimes for his friends. But if Elvis was to be a player in the future of rock 'n' roll then the universe would have to move him out of the tiny nowhere town of Tupelo and into the flourishing city of Memphis, Tennessee.

Heading north, Vernon moved his family there in 1948. The move was optimistic and the Presleys were hopeful for fresh new opportunities. The Second World War was over, unemployment was down to 3.9% and Columbia Records had just introduced the 33 1/3 LP (long-playing) record. For Elvis this move to Memphis was coincidentally perfectly timed, as the musical young man now found himself living in the heart of the blues and country

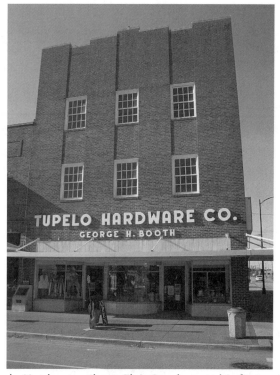

Tupelo Hardware where Elvis Presley got his first guitar
(Thomas R Machnitzki)

worlds, a musical jumble that teenage Elvis soaked up like a sponge. In Memphis, the Presleys lived in a downtown apartment complex provided by the welfare housing authority. Although now living in a notorious housing project, Elvis couldn't have been happier as he quickly made friends in this new town full of music. Almost every night Elvis and his posse wandered to nearby Beale Street and the Ellis Auditorium where he heard an assortment of gospel and blues acts both national and local. A teenage Elvis even saw famous blues players like Muddy Waters and B.B. King jam live on Beale Street, and whatever music wasn't playing live could be found on the radio. Famous Memphis DJ's like Dewey Phillips were playing cutting-edge blues tracks while Sonny Boy Williamson and Howlin' Wolf had the still-evolving country genre covered. Elvis would listen to the radio late into the night, and usually by the next afternoon his mother would be telling him about

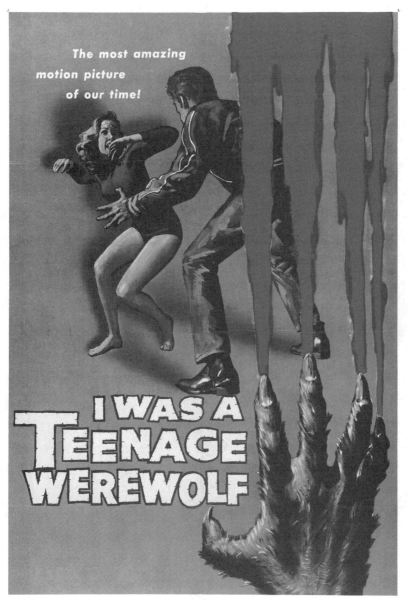

I was a Teenage Werewolf movie poster 1957 (Reynold Brown)

that night's sleepwalking episode or recounting the nightmare he was having. Elvis suffered from sleepwalking and nightmares all his life, but these episodes were extremely prevalent during his teenage years. Scientists recently linked these symptoms to people gifted with high levels of creative and artistic abilities. Pioneering sleep psychiatrist Dr. Ernest Hartmann believed that sufferers from nightmares were more likely to be creative people and artists. Hartmann believed this "vulnerability" came from the artist's ability to be touched by the world, experiencing life and all of its ecstasies and pain. He writes in his book *The Nightmare*: "One important aspect of what makes a person an artist is having a psychological makeup of thin boundaries, which includes the ability to experience and take in a great deal from inside and outside, to experience one's own inner life in a very direct fashion, and (sometimes an unwanted ability) to experience the world more directly, more painfully than others." [4]

The novels *Dr. Jekyll and Mr. Hyde*, *Frankenstein* and *Dracula* were all inspired by nightmares suffered by the authors. A professor of child psychiatry at the Washington University School of Medicine in St. Louis, Dr. E. James Anthony, agreed with Dr.

Teenage Elvis with friend (AFP/Getty)

Hartmann's findings saying: "The kind of person who has many nightmares seems to be hypersensitive in general. Virginia Woolf used the term 'thin-skinnedness' to describe it. She herself was the prototype: highly stress-sensitive, unable to handle everyday situations others would toss off. Like her, many such people become highly creative. They seem to do well as long as they have a creative outlet."

At Humes High, newcomer Elvis was honing his creative outlets while reinventing himself at the same time. An impressionable teenager of the 1950s, Elvis was inspired by James Dean and Marlon Brando, but set himself apart with oddball fashion statements like striped dress pants, bolero jackets, wavy duckbill hair and sideburns. He shopped for most of his clothes down on Beale Street and would have made for a stylish pimp dressed for the player's ball when most boys his age were rocking crew cuts, t-shirts and Levi's. Much like "Johnny Guitar" the six-string-wielding hero of the silver screen that inspired Jimi Hendrix, Elvis was a guitar-slinging curiosity who took his guitar everywhere, including high school. When some tough kids set out to beat him up and smash his guitar, Red West, football stud, lifelong friend and bodyguard, set the boys straight with a few right crosses and nobody ever bothered Elvis at school again. When Elvis wasn't at school or practicing music he was doing other normal teenage activities like making out with chicks, reading comics and working odd jobs to help out his impoverished family. In April 1953 Elvis performed in the annual Humes High minstrel show, and the kids that didn't know Elvis could sing were in for a huge surprise.

Elvis later reflected, "Nobody knew I even sang. It was amazing how popular I became after that." Elvis graduated from high school later that year, but dreams of supporting himself on a musician's salary were put in check by his father's stern words of advice regarding the life of a starving musician and not knowing any guitar player worth a lick. Heeding Vernon's recommendation, and committed to helping his family out financially, 18-year-old Elvis eventually got a job driving a truck for Crown Electric. By the summer of '53 Elvis had passed by the Sun Records recording studio so many times he no longer could bear it, and on July 18, eighteen-year-old Elvis paid $3.95 out of his own pocket to make a two-sided record.

Sun Records was operated by Sam Phillips, the first white producer to record black artists in Memphis, and who like Elvis was passionate about music, especially R&B "race music" that some white people liked, but weren't sure whether they should or not. Unfortunately Phillips wasn't around to record Elvis' very first demo session which contained the very green-sounding songs by the Ink Spots, "My Happiness" and "That's When Your Heartaches Begin," wherein Elvis croons like a mixture of Memphis singers Bill Keeny and Jimmy Sweeney. The job of recording his first ever studio performance went to Phillips' tireless secretary Marion Keisker. She curiously took note of Elvis' flamboyant clothes and long, slicked-back hair, asking him what type of music he sang and who he sounded like. Elvis prophetically answered, "I don't sound like nobody," which piqued her curiosity even more.

An excited Elvis left the studio with a freshly-pressed wax of his recordings and hoped that Phillips would eventually hear the songs and ask him back. Phillips never called, and Elvis continued to work as a journeyman electrician for Crown Electric. By late

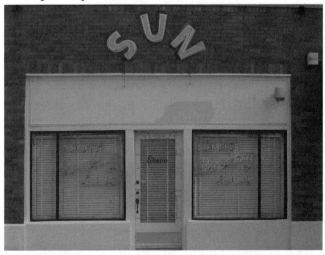

Sun Studios in Memphis, Tennessee (jglazer75)

August, Elvis was still plucking on his guitar and doing any live gig that came along, all the while wondering if his musical ambitions were just a pipe dream. Around the same time, the mysterious Colonel Tom Parker, a legendary Nashville manager, was let go by his sole client—the number-one selling country artist of the time Eddy, Arnold.

On January 4, 1954 Elvis decided to give it another shot and went back to Sun to cut another acetate record. This time recorded by Phillips, he sang "I'll Never Stand in Your Way" and "It Wouldn't Be the Same Without You." Although initially unimpressed, Phillips wrote down Elvis' phone number and address just in case

Ampex 300 1/2" 3-channel recorder used at Sun Studios (jglazer75)

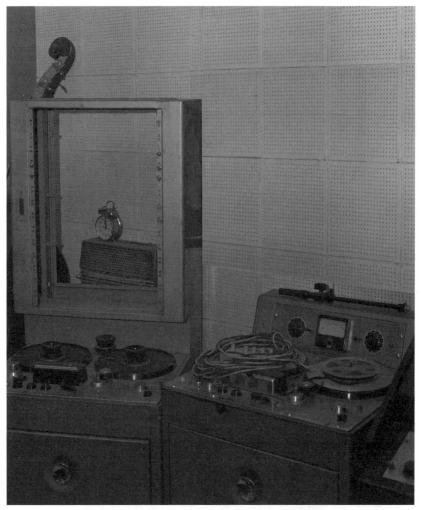

Sun Studios reel to reels (H. Michael Miley)

they needed him (which he doubted). Four months had passed without a word from Phillips, and Elvis was again trying to gig and auditioning for local bands. Presley auditioned as band leader at the Hi-Hat club downtown, but the owner turned him down. It seemed that a life in music wasn't in the cards and Elvis would be traversing the career path of Southern truck driver.

But fate intervened when Peer Music of Nashville sent Phillips an acetate demo of the ballad "Without You," and told him to track down the singer or re-record it with someone else. Unable to identify the singer and encouraged by Marion Keisker's zeal for the promising young truck driver, Phillips decided to allow Elvis to record the new ballad. On June 26, 1954, a typical muggy Southern summer afternoon, Elvis got a call from Marion Keisker asking if he could "be here by three."—"I was there by the time she hung up the phone," Elvis famously commented.

Despite his best efforts, Elvis failed to nail the song, but when Phillips asked him to sing whatever he wanted, a hopeful Elvis enthusiastically peeled off numbers from his extensive repertoire of country and gospel ballads. After the session was over, Elvis expressed his desire to start a band. Phillips suggested he get together with Scotty Moore, a promising young guitarist playing with various local country groups throughout Tennessee. Elvis didn't waste any time, and dropped by to see Moore during a backyard celebration on the fourth of July dressed in a flashy pink-and-white-striped suit. Moore was taken aback at the kid's flamboyant look, but the two instantly gelled when it came to the music. Moore introduced Elvis to bass player Bill Black, and the next day the trio met at Sun Records and spent a long, hot Memphis afternoon searching for a sound that clicked. The results would have a catastrophic effect on the future of pop culture.

Although the first songs they tried recording that day didn't sit well with Phillips, Elvis, guitarist Scotty Moore and bassist Bill Black finally stumbled on something special while fooling around with a sped-up version of Arthur "Big Boy" Crudup's "That's All Right," forcing Phillips to jump out of his chair and ask, "What was that?" They didn't really know, so they just played it over and over until Phillips was satisfied with the recording. It was exactly the style of music Sam Phillips had been searching for, and with Elvis he could now realize his dream of producing a white boy with that "Negro sound," an experiment that he prophetically predicted could make millions of dollars. But unfortunately for Phillips, he wouldn't be the one cashing in.

Phillips took several acetates of the session to DJ Dewey Phillips (no relation) to play on his *Red, Hot, and Blue* radio program at

WHBQ, and when the listeners heard it they went wild. "That's All Right" was first played on Memphis radio July 8, 1954 and DJ Dewey was kept busy answering phones all night demanding he play the song again. Less than a week later, Phillips had received more than 6,000 advance orders for Presley's first single "That's All Right/Blue Moon of Kentucky" which was released on July 19, 1954. That fall both songs began to chart across the South where a 19-year-old Elvis became a regional phenomenon.

With Moore and Black added to his touring line up, Elvis now had his very own full-fledged band, and over the next year the trio released four more singles and toured extensively across the South. They appeared regularly on the Louisiana Hayride, which was the biggest stage rival to the Grand Ole Opry at the time. They had originally auditioned for the Opry in October 1954, but having failed to impress the people in charge they were not invited back. Jim Denny, talent and booking manager for the Opry, infamously told Presley that he should "go back to driving a truck." Undeterred, Presley and the boys continued to tour, still riding the wave from their initial hit "That's All Right" while the press comically attempted to explain the kid's sound.

Elvis was referred to as everything from a "hillbilly singer," "a young rural rhythm talent," a "white man...singing Negro rhythms with a rural flavor," to "a young man with a boppish approach to hillbilly music." It wouldn't be long before other rockabilly and country singers began showing up on the doorsteps of Sun Records, hoping that Phillips could work the same magic with them. Phillips' musical contributions at Sun Records and the effect they had on the development of rock 'n' roll should never be underestimated. Phillips eventually recorded Jerry Lee Lewis, Carl Perkins, Roy Orbison, Charlie Feathers, Billy Lee Riley, and 'the man in black' Johnny Cash. In his autobiography, Cash recalled the very first time that he met Elvis, then the reigning Memphis wunderkind:

> The first time I saw Elvis, singing from a flatbed truck at a Katz drugstore opening on Lamar Avenue, two or three hundred people, mostly teenage girls, had

come out to see him. With just one single to his credit, he sang those two songs over and over. That's the first time I met him. Vivian and I went up to him after the show, and he invited us to his next date at the Eagle's Nest... I remember Elvis' show at the Eagle's Nest as if were yesterday. The date was a blunder, because the place was an adult club where teenagers weren't welcome, and so Vivian and I were two of only a dozen or so patrons, fifteen at the most. All the same, I thought Elvis was great. He sang *That's All Right, Mama* and *Blue Moon of Kentucky* once again (and again) plus some black blues songs and a few numbers like *Long Tall Sally*, and he didn't say much. He didn't have to, of course; his charisma alone kept everyone's attention. Elvis was such a nice guy, and so talented and charismatic—he had it all—that some people just couldn't handle it and reacted with jealousy. He was a kid when I worked with him. He was nineteen years old, and he loved cheeseburgers, girls, and his mother, not necessarily in that order (it was more like his mother, then girls, then cheeseburgers). Personally, I liked cheeseburgers and I had nothing against his mother, but the girls were the thing. He had so many girls after him that whenever he was working with us, there were always plenty left over. We had a lot of fun. We had a lot of fun in general, not just with the girls. It was nice that we could make a living at it, but every one of us would have done it for free. And you know, Elvis was so good. Every show I did with him, I never missed the chance to stand in the wings and watch. We all did. He was that charismatic. [5]

As Elvis continued to scorch a trailblazing path across the South, his hopes of going national were at the mercy of an unassuming songwriter, a shrewd business manager and a lonely soul who committed suicide deep in the entrails of the Magic City.

2.
Heartbreak — on through Hotel

Hanging in a crystal tree
A love light shines for all to see
'Cause in our hearts we know the way it goes
Sharing all that we can give
And living all that we can live
With freedom as our only cornerstone
Mystic traveler, he's the unraveler
And he will always bring you safely home
Mystic traveler, he's the unraveler
And when he takes your heart, you're not alone
And when he takes your heart, you're not alone
Time is on our side I feel
The light of truth will soon reveal

— Dave Mason

Be not deceived; God is not mocked: for whatsoever a man soweth, that shall he also reap.— Galatians 6:7

From the time I was a kid, I always knew that something was going to happen to me. Didn't know exactly what.— Elvis

Miami is a world-famous mecca of sun, sand, sex, fun and outlandish decadence. It's also a very dark town, haunted by real-life zombies, third world-esque poverty and a long history of racial segregation and violence. Because of this exotic mix, Miami boasts an impressive musical resume, birthing a mix of pirates, tropical wanderers and wayward sons that over the decades have created some of the most groundbreaking, influential and varying musical styles. With a long history of music innovation and violence, it's no wonder that Miami shows up as the spark that helped create rock 'n' roll—in the form of a suicide note.

33

Elvis is Alive: The Complete Conspiracy

Late one night in some faded neon Art Deco beach hotel, an anonymous man killed himself leaving behind only a crumbled note in one of his jeans pockets. On the note were the words, "I walk a lonely street"—his last ode to a cruel world. Little did he know his sacrificial death would soon give birth to a whole new generation of music lovers. His unidentified corpse was shown on the cover of the *Miami Herald* with the headline asking, "Do You Know This Man?" When exactly this suicide happened can't be confirmed, and a search of the *Miami Herald* digital archives hasn't provided any help. We know that it was sometime in 1955 when steel guitar player, singer-songwriter and failed dishwasher repairman Tommy Durden read the *Herald* suicide article while working a gig in Jacksonville, Florida. Durden believed the suicide note's line had a dark blues quality, and scribbled it down as a future song lyric. He showed the article and the lyric to his friend Mae Boren Axton, herself a songwriter, TV personality, radio host, publicist and schoolteacher. Mae was immediately drawn to the lyric, deciding that naturally, at the end of a lonely street one would find a "Heartbreak Hotel." With that verse, a light bulb of creativity exploded in the warm Florida air.

Mae wrote the rest of the lyrics while Durden worked out the melodies on his guitar. Within an hour, the duo had composed one of the most important songs in the history of music. But Mae was more than just a schoolteacher and part-time songwriter; she was a visionary who saw the 'big picture' before anybody else. That 'picture' of course was Elvis Presley, and way before the Colonel turned him into a money-making machine, Mae Axton was convinced that Elvis was going to be the biggest thing to hit America since the Model-T Ford. She first encountered Elvis during a tour she helped set up in Jacksonville, Florida when the relatively unknown Memphis singer was a last minute replacement booked to open for country recording star Hank Snow. As Elvis began his set, Mae quietly blended in with the crowd at the Gator Bowl, and watched in awe as 20-year old Elvis completely blew the audience away with his mix of hillbilly swag, bluesy crooning and pelvis shaking lunacy. After his performance, teenage girls chased Elvis back to the dressing room while managing to completely tear off the young stud's shirt. The 40-year-old Mae had never seen anything like that in her entire life. Nobody had. She quickly helped get Elvis booked for a return show on July 28, 1955, which saw excessive lines of teenage girls waiting to get inside and irate local preachers screaming about the dangers of Elvis and his shaking hips. After another smashing performance, Mae interviewed Elvis for a local radio station, and during the interview Elvis acknowledged Mae's influence in helping get his first record "That's All Right Mama" radio airplay in Florida. He said, "Well, thank you very much, Mae, and I'd like to personally thank you for really promoting my record, because you really have done a wonderful job, and I really do appreciate it because if you don't have people backing you, people pushing you, well you might as well quit." [6]

After the interview, Mae boldly declared to Elvis that she would write his first number one hit. After she concluded the "Heartbreak" writing session with Durden, a local country singer named Glenn Reeves stopped by for a visit and was immediately put to work by Mae. She asked Reeves to record a demo of the song with her tape recorder in the style of Elvis Presley. Reeves wasn't a fan, but being a good friend, did the song anyway. The fact that Reeves even knew who Elvis was, is a testament to how much buzz the King had created for himself in the South. After finishing the song, Reeves thought "Heartbreak Hotel" was weird and that Elvis "wouldn't go far," declined any credit or association with the song. Mae had no intention of ever using Reeves anyway; she just wanted something to show Elvis in the hope that he would record the song. She approached the popular country duo The Wilburn Brothers and offered them a chance to record a better quality version of "Heartbreak Hotel" but the duo declined, calling the song "strange and almost morbid." With no choice but to hunt down the kid on her own, she headed to Nashville where Elvis was being honored as the most promising male country star of 1955 at the annual Country Music Disc Jockey Convention.

By this time, Colonel Tom Parker had weaseled his way into becoming Elvis' manager, and shortly after Thanksgiving of 1955, secured for Elvis a record deal at RCA. Since Mae had worked with Tom before as a publicist in the early '50s she was on familiar terms with the Memphis slickster. It's even rumored that Mae is the only person in the world that the notorious Colonel Tom Parker ever apologized to. After talking with Tom about the song she wanted Elvis to record she was told where to find the kid, and headed out in the rain toward the Andrew Jackson Hotel.

Elvis was relaxing in his room and in a jovial mood when Mae showed up with her tape-recorded demo. Upon hearing the rough-sounding tape Elvis shouted, "Hot dog, Mae! Play it again!" He was mesmerized as they played the track about ten times in a row. Elvis said the song reminded him of Roy Brown's "Hard Luck Blues" and agreed to record a version. Mae was delighted, and the next day they sat down with the Colonel to hammer out a deal. Though the team of Mae and Durden are responsible for penning the song, Elvis gets credit on the finished record as a third writer. It's common knowledge that the Colonel often insisted that his boy get co-writing credits in exchange for cutting a song, as a way of

Elvis in Arkansas (Mary Lou Campbell)

Elvis performing in Arkansas (Mary Lou Campbell)

securing a steady stream of publishing checks for the two of them. However in this case, Mae was so confident "Heartbreak" would establish Elvis as a star that she insisted on a shared credit to help Elvis buy a house for his mother.

With formalities out of the way, Elvis began to rehearse the song and added it to his live repertoire, changing one line of the lyric (from "they pray to die" to "they could die") while

Elvis with girls in Arkansas (Mary Lou Campbell)

37

performing the song for the first time in Swifton, Arkansas on December 9. The small club was packed with over 200 people and Elvis, oozing with confidence after signing with RCA, rocked the club to its knees. The club's owner and everyone there could sense that something special was happening.

The 20-year-old Elvis was already a regional star but he had yet to appear on national television. That night in the Arkansas club, Elvis burned through his Sun catalogue, a few covers, and then introduced his new song in that familiar Southern drawl: "I've got this brand new song and it's gonna be my first hit." His words were prophetic.

A month later Elvis entered the recording studios at RCA, where he was scheduled to record five songs in two days. The studio at 1525 McGavock Street was RCA's first_permanent recording facility in Nashville, a town still years away from becoming the recording center of the musical universe. Surprisingly, at that time there were only a handful of studios in town. It was January 10, 1956 and Elvis Presley, who had just turned 21 two days prior was ready to begin recording his debut single for RCA. Mae was also present during the session, as she was interested in watching Elvis record live, and curious as to how her song would end up sounding. Elvis was joined in the studio by legendary Nashville guitarist Chet Atkins on rhythm guitar and future Grammy winner Floyd Cramer on piano, along with gospel singers The Jordanaires.

During that first session, RCA was anxious to recreate the "slapback" echo effect that Sam Phillips had created at Sun. Chet and engineer Bob Farris created a pseudo echo chamber by setting up a speaker at one end of a long hallway and a microphone at the other end and recording the echo live. It sounded strange to hear it as they were recording live because at Sun studios Sam used to add the effect afterwards. This technique failed to add anything special to the first two songs they recorded ("I Got a Woman" and "Money Honey") but when they tried it out on "Heartbreak Hotel" goose pimples suddenly appeared on everybody's skin.

The heavy overdubbing of echo and the drummer's rim shots

Elvis at RCA's Mcgavock St. Studio (Don Cravens)

created a powerful atmosphere of upbeat despair that effortlessly matched Elvis' heart-rending vocal. It was a perfect blend of haunting lyrics and ghostly music set to the penetrating crooning of a man destined for greatness. During the opening lines to each verse when Elvis sings a capella, his voice is penetrating, dejected, and completely captures the alienation of disaffected youth. The dark track sounded more like it belonged on a Doors album than a lead single for RCA in 1956. The gloomy song was markedly different from anything Elvis had done previously at Sun Records, and when his former label boss Sam Phillips heard an acetate from the Nashville session, he called it a "morbid mess." Biographer Donald Clarke writes:

> The sound quality of that first session was not good, and 'Heartbreak Hotel' is the worst of them all. Chet Atkins played rhythm guitar and Floyd Cramer was added on piano, together with an entirely unnecessary vocal trio led by Gordon Stoker, lead singer of the Jordanaires. Scotty Moore's guitar sounds exceptionally, irritatingly tinny, Cramer is too prominent and the whole track

39

Elvis is Alive: The Complete Conspiracy

Elvis signing autographs after leaving RCA's Mcgavock
St. Studio (Don Cravens)

sounds like it was made underwater in a breadbox. It was a disgraceful recording for 1956 but a good song for Presley.[7]

On hearing the new songs, the RCA executives in New York freaked out and wanted to scrap the sessions. They told producer Steve Sholes to turn around and head straight back to Nashville to re-record the tracks. Sholes later stated, "They all told me it didn't sound like anything, it didn't sound like his other records and I'd better not release it, better go back and record it again." But Elvis was

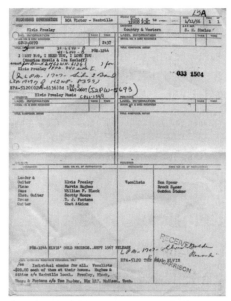

Misdated RCA recording sheet (Ger Rijff)

Elvis with first Gold Record (Don Cravens)

unfazed and begged the grey-haired executives to trust his instincts and release "Heartbreak Hotel" as a single, promising that if it sank he would be at their mercy for any song they wanted out of him. Elvis had that Southern charm, and he had it in spades. The RCA brass relented and forged ahead with the release, albeit with sizeable suspicions. Elvis clearly believed in it, certain that the song was the right one to catapult him into the big time.

It was properly mastered and released as a 45 single with the B-side "I Was the One" on January 27, 1956, and went nowhere despite Elvis making his network television debut on the Dorsey Brothers Stage Show. For the first month of its release "Heartbreak" barely registered on the pop charts, which seemed to prove that the RCA executives were right. But that all changed when Elvis finally had the chance to perform the song on the popular Milton Berle Show. This performance, from the deck of the aircraft carrier *USS Hancock* in San Diego, California, shot Elvis to superstardom. His good looks, unique voice and swiveling hips sent the blonde-haired, blue-eyed California girls into a frenzy of screams, faints and tears. The men had never seen anything like it, and the San

Elvis fans (Charles Trainor)

Diego Police Chief announced that if Elvis ever returned to his city and performed again in the way that he had, he would be jailed for disorderly conduct. Like an unexpected meteor blast, Elvis had hit the mainstream.

A fateful string of television appearances (a new medium) undoubtedly helped propel "Heartbreak Hotel" to the number one spot on Billboard's best-seller list 45 days after its release, where it stayed number one for eight weeks. The song also reached number one on the country charts and number three on the R&B charts. It became Elvis Presley's first gold record selling more than a million copies, just as Mae Axton had predicted. Considering this is the song that really introduced rock to the mainstream (white public) it's amazing how dark the lyrics really are...

Well, since my baby left me, I found a new place to dwell.
It's down at the end of lonely street at heartbreak hotel.
You make me so lonely baby,
I get so lonely, I get so lonely I could die.
And although it's always crowded, you still can find some room.
Where broken hearted lovers do cry away their gloom.
Well, the bell hop's tears keep flowin' and the desk clerk's dressed in black.
Well they been so long on lonely street they ain't ever gonna look back.

"Heartbreak Hotel" put Elvis on the map, and helped forever alter the landscape of popular culture. He would perform the song during most of his live shows between 1956 and 1977, including a blistering rendition on his 1968 comeback special. Elvis performed it for the last time on May 29, 1977 at the Civic Center in Baltimore, Maryland. The song and alternative takes have been released on almost every Presley compilation album since the '60s and is one of the most influential songs of all time. It single-handedly ushered in the era of rock 'n' roll and influenced every key rock artist in its wake. John Lennon recalled the night that he met Elvis and the impact the King had on his life:

Before Elvis there was nothing. When I first heard "Heartbreak Hotel," I could hardly make out what was being said. It was just the experience of hearing it and having my hair stand on end. We'd never heard American voices singing like that. They always sung like Sinatra or enunciate very well. Suddenly, there's this hillbilly hiccupping on tape echo and all this bluesy stuff going on... there's only one person in the United States we ever wanted to meet... not that he wanted us. And we met him last night... It was very exciting, we were all nervous as hell, and we met him in his big house in L.A. He had lots of guys around him and he had pool tables! Maybe a lot of American houses are like that, but it seemed amazing to us. It was like a nightclub. He had his TV going all the time, which is what I do; we always have TV on. We never watch it—it's just there with no sound on, and we listen to records. In front of the TV, he had a massive amplifier with a bass plugged into it, and he was up playing bass all the time with the picture up on the TV. So we just got in there and played with him. We all plugged in whatever was around, and we played and sang. He had a jukebox, like I do, but I think he had all his hits on it. But if I'd made as many as him, maybe I'd have all mine on. At first we couldn't make him out. I asked him if he was preparing new ideas for his next film and he drawled, "Ah sure am. Ah play a country boy with a guitar who meets a few gals along the way, and ah sing a few songs." We all looked at one another. Finally Presley and Colonel Parker laughed and explained that the only time they departed from that formula—for Wild in the Country—they lost money. It was nice meeting Elvis. He was just Elvis, you know? He seemed normal to us, and we were asking about his making movies and not doing any personal appearances or TV. I think he enjoys making movies so much, we couldn't stand not doing personal appearances, we'd get bored—we get bored quickly. He says he misses it a bit. We never talked about anything else—we just played music. If there hadn't been an Elvis, there wouldn't have been the Beatles. [8]

The Rolling Stones' guitarist Keith Richards claims that upon hearing "Heartbreak Hotel" he was never the same. He writes:

Good records just get better with age. But the one that really turned me on, like an explosion one night, listening to Radio Luxembourg on my little radio when I was supposed to be in bed and asleep, was "Heartbreak Hotel." That was the stunner. I'd never heard it before, or anything like it. I'd never heard of Elvis before. It was almost as if I'd been waiting for it to happen. When I woke up the next day I was a different guy. [9]

With "Heartbreak" a certifiable smash, Elvis Presley was on his way to superstardom. Over the years he begged Mae to write more songs for him, but feeling she could never top "Heartbreak" Mae declined, content that her initial hunch about Elvis was right. Mae continued to write through the '60s and '70s while maintaining a career as a schoolteacher and community activist, proud to have set Elvis on his way but completely nonchalant about writing one of the most groundbreaking songs ever. In a 1982 interview, the song's co-writer, Tommy Durden, said that the song, "has paid the rent for more than 20 years." Citing its cultural significance, the Grammys inducted the song into their Hall of Fame. When then presidential candidate Bill Clinton (later called "the first black president" by Nobel laureate Toni Morrison) made his famous appearance on *The Arsenio Hall Show* in 1992, he chose "Heartbreak Hotel" to play on his sax. He killed it, got the crowd hyped and secured the gig for the presidency. And to the deserted soul who took his own life in Miami, never knowing that his suicide note ("I walk a lonely street") would forever change the world by helping shape and create the phenomenon of rock 'n' roll—Thank You. Sadly, your loss was our gain. But as Elvis mania swept the nation Uncle Sam was curiously lurking in the background and eager to recruit the kid with the dangerous hips.

3.
Elvis Joins the Army (Monarch Butterfly)

Just before the battle, mother,
I am thinking most of you,
While upon the field we're watching
With the enemy in view.
Comrades brave are 'round me lying,
Filled with thoughts of home and God
For well they know that on the morrow,
Some will sleep beneath the sod.

CHORUS:
Farewell, mother, you may never
Press me to your heart again,
But, oh, you'll not forget me, mother,
If I'm numbered with the slain.

Oh, I long to see you, mother,
And the loving ones at home,
But I'll never leave our banner,
Till in honor I can come.
Tell the traitors all around you
That their cruel words we know,
In every battle kill our soldiers
By the help they give the foe.

Hark! I hear the bugles sounding,
'Tis the signal for the fight,
Now, may God protect us, mother,
As He ever does the right.
Hear the "Battle-Cry of Freedom,"
How it swells upon the air,
Oh, yes, we'll rally 'round the standard,
Or we'll perish nobly there.

— George F. Root (Written during the American Civil War)

47

One who is righteous is a guide to his neighbor, but the way of the wicked leads them astray.— Proverbs 12:26

Ambition is a dream with a V8 engine.— Elvis

Elvis was a full-blown superstar by the time he was drafted into the Army. Most adults thought it was a good thing for him to be straightened up and shipped out far and away from their teenage daughters. His overly sexual dance moves had caused national outrage while capturing the hearts of teenage girls everywhere. He wasn't trying to be super sexy, it's just that he was so nervous that his knees started to rumble and he just went with it. But to many parents and religious leaders in 1956, Elvis' erotic stage antics and strange rock music were just way too much to handle. Elvis soon turned 21 and became eligible to be drafted; he began to worry about where his career might end up. Meanwhile Uncle Sam was waiting in the wings, with a drooling mouth. Elvis was such a phenomenon that not even the military had seen him coming. Now they wanted the boy, and wanted him bad.

But here's where Colonel Tom Parker's managerial genius comes in. Parker knew the Army Special Services would immediately send Elvis out on USO tours and goodwill missions where the kid would be required to perform for free. Each performance recording of these tours would be sold throughout the world, and only the armed forces would profit. But a cunning Parker was in no way willing to allow anyone, even Uncle Sam, to enjoy Presley's talents for free. He persuaded Elvis to enlist as a grunt, just an ordinary E-1 soldier, and assured Elvis that this move would earn him the respect of many of his fellow soldiers and the older people back home, who had previously viewed him negatively. This is exactly what happened. Elvis breezed through boot camp while thousands of girls cried over his shredded locks.

The Colonel was already preparing enough material for the two years Elvis was going to be away. The relationship he shared with Elvis had become legendary over the years. His savvy move using

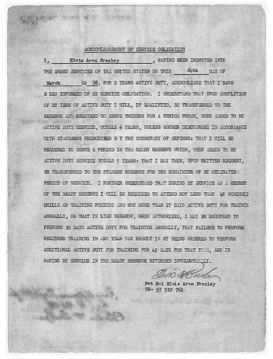

Elvis at RCA's Mcgavock St. Studio (Don Cravens)

television (a new medium) to put Elvis on the map is iconic. Elvis was basically still a kid when he put his faith in the Colonel, and the Colonel paid off big time, securing Elvis number one records and movie roles. The Colonel is perhaps the greatest manager of all time thanks to Elvis, but he wasn't a "Colonel" or even American. He was born Andreas Cornelis van Kuijk in Breda, Holland, an illegal immigrant in the USA with fake papers, a fake name and no desire to travel abroad ever again, a situation that prevented Elvis from achieving one of his true dreams—a tour of Europe.

The Colonel did serve in the US Army on a base in Hawaii for a little while before going AWOL, and then spent some time in a military prison before being shipped to a mental institution suffering from psychosis. Deemed a psychopath, he was given his walking papers by the Army in 1933. Afterward, Parker made his way to Florida and worked various carnival jobs before making his first foray into artist management with up-and-coming country star Eddy Arnold in the late '40s. With a 25% contract, Parker hit the big time as Arnold shot straight to the top of the charts. He repeated this feat with Hank Snow, and the Colonel became known as the "Memphis Slickster," a respected pioneer of early management. It wouldn't be long before Elvis would be his sole client, but Elvis' mother couldn't stand Parker. The only reason she let him manage Elvis was because Hank Snow luckily

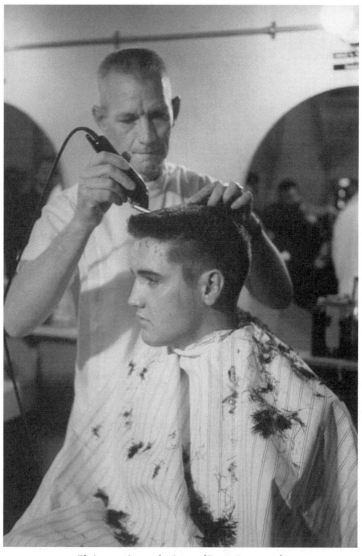

Elvis getting a haircut (Don Cravens)

happened to be her favorite singer.

Despite Parker's managerial talent, it was Elvis' dynamic performances that struck a chord with teenagers in Middle America. After all, Elvis was one of them, and just a teenager himself. A product of his time and exceptional timing, Elvis perfectly fitted the need for a post-war teenage star capable of changing popular music and pushing it forward. A whole new utopia of pop culture was spawned by the talents of Elvis in the television era. It was as if the universe guided him specifically in order to achieve this monumental event. The dynamic impact of his good looks, singing voice and explosive creativity helped fuel the engine that would drive the Presley Empire. But that empire owes at least half to the managerial genius of the Colonel, a man who had a strong mental hold over an impressionable Elvis. Some have even suggested that the Colonel was a former intelligence agent and he was using mind control techniques. However, proof of these claims does not exist.

While the Colonel was taking care of business, Elvis worried that rock 'n'roll was a fad, and that by the time the Army got through with him he would be back to being broke. After being poor his entire life and then suddenly coming into more money than he ever imagined, Elvis was plagued by nightmares of waking up poor over and over again until his demise. Now 22, he personally wrote to the Memphis Draft Board requesting a deferment, so he could finish filming the movie *King Creole*. When the board approved, it was bombarded by angry letters and negative press decrying the "special treatment" that Presley had received. To his credit, Elvis gave the performance of his career and solidified his true future potential as a serious actor. Of course, the Colonel squandered this talent and bored the hell out of Elvis by placing him in the same moronic teen movies for a decade straight. He even refused to allow Elvis a role in *West Side Story*, a movie that has since become iconic, and one can imagine how great Elvis could have been in it. The Colonel also failed to let Elvis act in the 1976 blockbuster *A Star is Born* with Barbra Streisand.

On "Black Monday," March 24, 1958, Elvis was inducted into

the Army and forced to wave for news crews from around the world before he and his fellow recruits were taken by bus to Fort Chaffee, Arkansas. Four days later Elvis was in basic training at Fort Hood, Texas and assigned to the A Company of the Second Armored Division's Tank Battalion. Elvis hated the Army, was homesick and worried about his career. He often called home in tears using his instructor Bill Norwood's phone. After surviving basic, Elvis rented a house off base, moving in his mother, father, grandmother, and a friend named Lamar Fike. But shortly after arriving in Texas, Gladys became ill. She had upped her alcohol and pill intake to cope with her son's sudden explosion of fame.

With a deteriorated liver ailing her, Gladys collapsed one night after a heated argument with Vernon. Elvis arranged for her and Vernon to be brought back to Memphis by train, where Gladys spent four days in the hospital. Elvis was granted emergency leave to deal with this unfortunate calamity. He kept a 36 hour vigil by her bedside, but as soon as he went home to sleep, his mother died from a heart attack brought on by cirrhosis of the liver. It's as if Gladys' spirit remained as long as Elvis was near.

The kid was shocked and devastated, barely able to express himself to the gathering press. Back at Graceland, he wandered around aimlessly and stared for long hours at the walls. Elvis attended his mother's funeral dazed and in disbelief, mentally unprepared having to deal with the devastating reality that his mother was now dead. He collapsed several times before, during, and after the service. His mother had always been the most important person in his life; he was a true mama's boy and with her now gone, felt as though everything he had worked for had been for naught. After the death of his mother, and now stationed in Germany, the young Elvis would be a perfect choice for the Army to experiment on with mind control using MK-Ultra tactics. The ingredients were already there. The death of his mother made Presley's mental state ripe for taking advantage of. Coincidently, according to Illuminati practices and occult philosophies, the sacrifice of a loved one is usually always involved in high satanic

Elvis lived at the Hotel Grunewald for the first four months in Germany
(Eva K)

experiments and events. The famous mind control operation MK-Ultra was in its infant stages during Presley's stay in Germany, and his assignment was in fact a pysop to prepare the Germans for a long-term American military presence there. Mind control operations such as MK-Ultra are real and have been recently declassified; even the Russians admitted to having spent over a billion dollars on mind control experiments and research dating back to the 1940s.[10]

Elvis lived with his family and a few friends off base in Bad Nauheim. While at home, he played the piano and listened to the Armed Forces Radio Network, whereas at work his duties ranged from night watch to driving sergeants around. During his stay in Germany Elvis began discovering the limits of amphetamines his body could handle, creating a dependency on prescription pills that lasted the rest of his life. Besides the pills, the Army also introduced Elvis to karate, one of his lifelong passions. Later, he

House on Gothestrasse 14 in Bad Nuheim (Chivista)

would incorporate karate moves into his musical routines. Despite being homesick and not cut out for Army life, Elvis did his best to fit in as a regular soldier—he even donated his pay to charity, purchased the base new TVs and bought extra sets of fatigues for everyone in his outfit.

By the time Elvis was discharged, he had earned the respect of his fellow soldiers, but whether he was mind controlled and reprogrammed is purely speculative. He had visited the hospital in Frankfurt a few times for a tonsillitis infection, but nothing stranger than that has been linkable to any mind control experiments. Besides, Elvis' mind was already blown enough. He had fallen for a 14-year-old girl who was the daughter of an intelligence officer—Priscilla Beaulieu.

While he was in Germany, the Elvis money machine continued to roll as RCA pumped out more songs. Between his induction and discharge, Elvis had ten Top 40 hits, including the number one selling "A Big Hunk o' Love." On February 11, 1960 Presley

Elvis Army discharge press conference discussion (James Whitmore)

received his sergeant stripes, and on March 1st the Army held a press conference announcing his discharge. During the conference he was asked why he chose to serve as a regular soldier rather than perform for the troops. He replied, "I was in a funny position. Actually, that's the only way it could be. People were expecting me to mess up, to goof up in one way or another. They thought I couldn't take it and so forth, and I was determined to go to any limits to prove otherwise, not only to the people who were wondering, but to myself."

The next day, with Priscilla in attendance, Presley waved goodbye to the fans and media of Germany and boarded a plane heading home to Memphis. En route, his plane stopped in Scotland to refuel marking the one and only time that Elvis would set foot in the UK. After his release from the Army, Elvis acquired a new fan base among an older age group, just like the Colonel had predicted. He was welcomed home with a television special hosted by Frank Sinatra at the decadent Fontainebleau on Miami Beach. Previously, Frank had talked a lot of dirt about Elvis and rock 'n' roll in general, but had changed his tune, mostly due to the fact that his teenage daughter Nancy was, like most girls her age, in love with Elvis. The kid even got to sing a duet with "Ol'

Blue Eyes" and the show was a smash, drawing the highest ratings numbers up to that point in television history. Elvis was back. Any concerns he had about his career were instantly quashed as he began to ascend higher up the ladder of superstardom than anyone thought possible. So high, in fact, that only pills and cheeseburgers could bring him down.

Elvis with Nixon (Ollie Atkins)

4.
Elvis Dies!

It was a rainy night
The night the king went down
Everybody was crying it seemed
Like sadness had surrounded the town

Me, I went to the liquor store
And I bought a bottle of wine and a bottle of gin
I played his records all night
Drinking with a close, close friend

Now some people say that that ain't right
And some people say nothing at all
But even in the darkest of night
You can always hear the king's call
You can always hear the king's call

— Phil Lynott

Every man's work shall be made manifest.

— Corinthians 3:13

I ain't no saint, but I've tried never to do anything that would hurt my family or offend God...I figure all any kid needs is hope and the feeling he or she belongs. If I could do or say anything that would give some kid that feeling, I would believe I had contributed something to the world.

— Elvis

Elvis was a prisoner of his own fame, and addled with many reasons to leave his life behind. Because of his incredible popularity, he was the recipient of several death threats, and he was concerned about the safety of his family. Sometimes when he wanted to leave Graceland, he would send out look-alikes to distract would-be followers. Elvis was also known to ride in the trunk of someone else's car to avoid detection. Once, when he fell ill in Las Vegas, he couldn't get proper medical attention because the hospital was overwhelmed by fans. At the time of his alleged death, Elvis was nearing the end of his career. He was 42, his hair was graying, he was grossly overweight, and his voice was starting to weaken. He was going downhill, and he was too proud to go out with a whimper. He would never want his fans to see him in such an unhealthy condition. Elvis had shown a fascination with death on several occasions. In the days leading up to his "death" he was reported to have visited funeral homes at odd hours of the night with close friends. Was he doing research?

One of Elvis' favorite books was *Autobiography of a Yogi*. One of the central themes of this book is the relinquishing of one's wealth and earthly possessions to achieve spiritual oneness. Elvis could do this, as well as address his other concerns of sanity and safety by faking his death and living in exile. Elvis had the means to fake his own death. He is accused of destroying himself with drugs, which he did, but Elvis was also a pharmaceutical expert. He took a lot of drugs, but he knew what he was doing and was extremely careful. He knew what drugs he could self-administer to create a deathlike state. Further, Elvis' experience with the martial arts was such that he could slow his heart rate and

Last known Photo of Elvis (Robert call)

breathing in order to fake death.

Faking one's own death would bring an end to the never-ending list of public demands that celebrities have no choice but to deal with. It would make sense that at 42, Elvis would be more than fed up with being the most famous man in the world. Keep in mind, faking your own death isn't actually illegal. It only becomes illegal if you cash in a life insurance claim when you're not dead. One of the biggest go-to pieces of evidence for those who

believe Elvis is alive is a Lloyd's of London insurance policy. Elvis supposedly purchased but never cashed out. This would support the hoax theory, since Elvis and his estate would be guilty of insurance fraud if they had. However, Elvis never purchased this particular policy, and already had multiple life insurance policies already in place for his family. Although the insurance claim has been debunked, there's still a lot more surprising things to look at, most of which can't easily be explained.

For instance Elvis was supposed to have been dead by 9 a.m. according to the doctor's estimation, but in fact he signed for a letter from Paul Lichter delivered around 9:45 a.m. And by the time his "dead" body arrived at Baptist Hospital, his mouth, throat and stomach had been mysteriously flushed. Elvis didn't even go to the nearest emergency room, Methodist Hospital South, which is standard operating procedure when dealing with life or death situations. Instead, Dr. Nick rerouted the King to the much more familiar Baptist Hospital, where chief medical examiner Dan Warlick was forbidden to take any autopsy pictures of Elvis. The only report to officially surface from Elvis' visit to the hospital is the medical examiner's report Postmortem #A77-160, which appears to be written by Elvis himself. Forensic experts have

Medical examiner's report 1 (The Presley Assignment)

come forward claiming the handwriting on the examiner's report is a perfect match. The weight is even listed at 170 pounds, which is exactly what Elvis listed as his weight on his Tennessee driver's license.

Elvis might have had a good laugh with the examiner's report, but the real juicy stuff would be found in the full autopsy report filed later, which remains the sole property of the Presley family. Because the autopsy report is a private medical record, it will not be released at any time, which sucks since apparently DNA from Elvis' 1975 liver biopsy doesn't match the DNA samples found in his autopsy report, according to the claims made by minister and Elvis fanboy, Bill Beeny. But since Beeny claims these samples were secretly removed from a controlled environment at Baptist Hospital by an unnamed doctor, and then mysteriously resurfaced decades later, it's kind of hard to take his story seriously.

Medical examiner's report 2 (The Presley Assignment)

Elvis dies (The Sun)

Elvis' official death certificate won't be released until 2027 and there are no existing photographs of Elvis' body during the autopsy. The postmortem report was already muddied by bizarre claims that Elvis was only 170 pounds when he died and that he had a huge scar running over his chest. We know Elvis was way fatter than 170 pounds (the firefighters that carried his body from Graceland to the ambulance estimated him to weigh around 255), and no, he didn't have any scars over his chest. And why did Warlick, the non-picture-taking Memphis medical examiner claim Elvis was found in the bathroom in a state of rigor mortis, while the police report said he was found in the bedroom merely "unconscious"? Bizarre as the autopsy and postmortem reports are, they were easily outdone by the funeral fit for a king.

Perhaps the most perplexing part of the Elvis-faked-his-own-

Elvis in casket (Enquirer)

death theory, and the one that makes the whole case baffling, was the public funeral. First off, why so soon? The funeral was only one day after Elvis' death, and the coffin weighed an amazing 900 pounds! How was the Presley family able to find a 900 pound coffin so fast? And why the hell would they need one? The spectacle of the mass of Elvis pallbearers struggling to carry the massive coffin is enough to make you laugh, or at least scratch your head in wonder. People who attended the funeral claim that areas around the coffin seemed colder, as if there were an air conditioner attached. Keeping the temperature low would be necessary if the body in the coffin was a wax replica of Elvis, a theory that might be true.

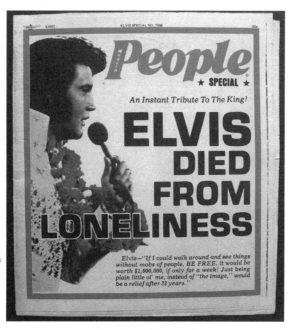

Elvis dies (People)

Elvis dies (Memphis Press)

Elvis how did he die? (People)

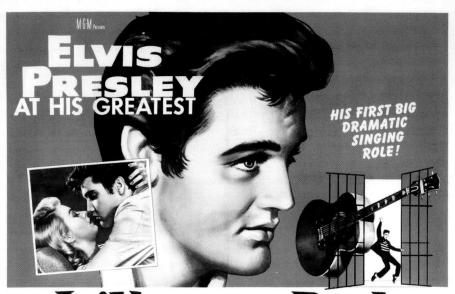

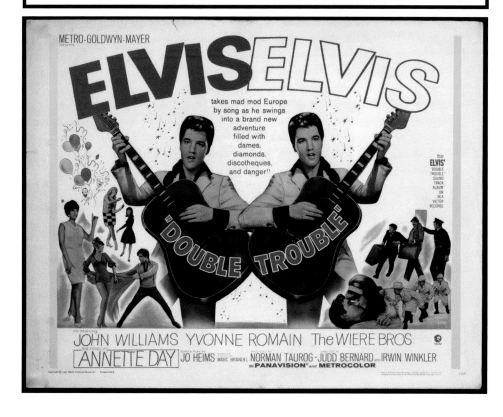

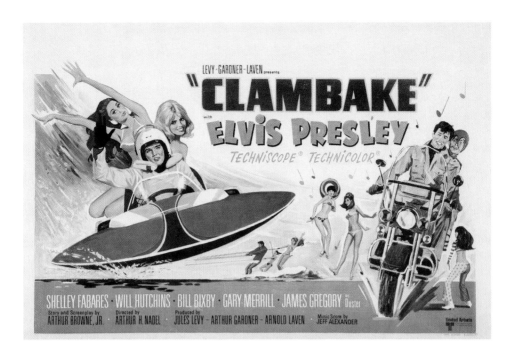

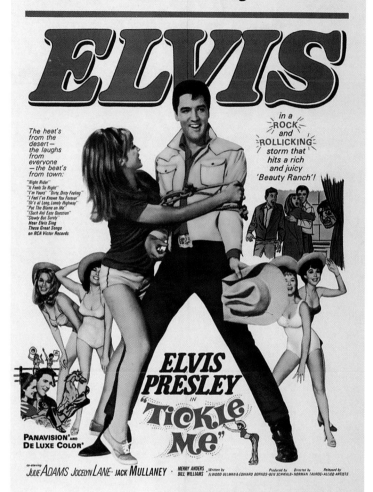

It's **Fun!**..... It's **Girls!**..... It's **Song!**..... It's **Color!**

ELVIS

The heat's from the desert — the laughs from everyone — the beat's from town:

"Night Rider"
"It Feels So Right"
"I'm Yours" "Dirty, Dirty Feeling"
"I Feel I've Known You Forever"
"It's a Long, Lonely Highway"
"Put The Blame on Me"
"(Such An) Easy Question"
"Slowly But Surely"
Hear Elvis Sing These Great Songs on RCA Victor Records

in a **ROCK** and **ROLLICKING** storm that hits a rich and juicy 'Beauty Ranch'!

ELVIS PRESLEY in "Tickle Me"

PANAVISION and DE LUXE COLOR

co-starring JULIE ADAMS · JOCELYN LANE · JACK MULLANEY · MERRY ANDERS · BILL WILLIAMS · Written by ELWOOD ULLMAN & EDWARD BERNDS · Produced by BEN SCHWALB · Directed by NORMAN TAUROG · Released by ALLIED ARTISTS

TWICE AS MUCH ELVIS AS EVER!

ELVIS PRESLEY in FUN IN ACAPULCO
HAL WALLIS' TECHNICOLOR

ELVIS PRESLEY in HAL WALLIS' "GIRLS! GIRLS! GIRLS!"
TECHNICOLOR

A DIFFERENT PRESLEY!

On his neck he wore the brand of a killer
On his hip he wore vengeance.

National General Pictures presents

ELVIS PRESLEY as CHARRO!

Co-starring INA BALIN · VICTOR FRENCH · BARBARA WERLE · SOLOMON STURGES · Introducing LYNN KELLOGG · TECHNICOLOR · PANAVISION

Executive Producer Harry Caplan · Music Charles Marquis Warren · Screenplay by Charles Marquis Warren · Story by Frederic Louis Fox · Produced and Directed by Charles Marquis Warren · Title Song sung by Elvis Presley · Music Composed and Conducted by Hugo Montenegro

Elvis on stunt motorcycle (AFP/Getty)

For example, the only known post-death picture of Elvis is the coffin pic. This photo clearly doesn't look like the fat Elvis that was living during that time. The nose is different and the hands are not rough enough. Elvis was a brick-busting sixth-degree black belt. One of the King's famous sideburns even appeared to be loose and falling off. A hairdresser later reported gluing the sideburn back on the body and beads of sweat, or drops from the glue or wax, were noticed by onlookers. The funeral wasn't even attended by Elvis' father or closest friends. They had a private gathering a week later.

Fans gather at Graceland on the day of Elvis' funeral
(photographer unknown)

Cameras weren't allowed at the funeral either. The famous photo of "dead" Elvis ran on the cover of the *National Enquirer* on September 6, 1977, two weeks after Elvis passed away. Who took the photo was the object of speculation for years, but it was later confirmed in a tell-all book by *Enquirer* editor Iain Calder that Elvis' cousin Billy Mann was paid $18,000 to sneak a photo of Elvis in his coffin. Elvis' cousin and confidant Billy Smith corroborated this claim.

There are also strange reports claiming a black helicopter was seen at the Graceland estate the day Elvis died. Did Elvis get on that helicopter? Monte Nicholson, a veteran with the Los Angeles Sheriff's Department writes in his novel *The Presley Arrangement* about a government helicopter hovering over Graceland, and finally landing in the back. Nicholson was informed there were pictures of Elvis getting on the helicopter during the early afternoon of August 16th. Larry Geller wrote in his memoir *If I Can Dream* that from his hotel window he saw multiple helicopters hovering above Graceland.

From the time Elvis was pronounced dead to when his body was viewed a little more than 24 hours later, an incredible, seemingly impossible, amount of activity took place. Autopsy and

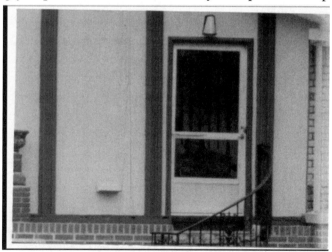

Elvis photographed two months after his "death"
(Lindahoodsigmontruth.com)

August 6, 1987

Mike Joseph
3200 McLeod Drive, Suite #293
Las Vegas, Nevada 89121

Dear Mr. Joseph:

We were happy to look at the enclosed 20 exposure color film.
The code "5035" identifies the film as being Kodacolor II.

In checking the film's emulsion number (#757) our records show
that the expiration date of the film was October, 1977. From
this information, we can conclude that the film was manufactured
18 months prior to that date, or approximately April, 1976.

The splice number 9839 at the end of the roll was placed on the
film by the original processor. Since we did not process the film,
we, of course, do not have records regarding the actual processing.
However, through a careful visual examination of the exposures,
the film does appear to have been processed correctly. We also see
no signs of the film having been altered in any way.

Thank you for contacting us, Mr. Joseph. If we can be of assistance
with any future photographic need, please let us know.

Sincerely,

Dixie Lee Mathews
Customer Services

EASTMAN KODAK COMPANY · COLOR PRINT AND PROCESSING
925 PAGE MILL ROAD · PALO ALTO, CALIFORNIA 94304 · 415 493-7200

Letter from Kodak verifying the negatives were unaltered
(Lindahoodsigmontruth.com)

embalming were completed, the body having been brought to Memphis Funeral Home around 8:00 p.m., 16 white limousines were ordered; a white Cadillac hearse was readied; a specially designed 900 pound casket was ordered and flown in; a casket blanket of 500 red roses was made; the security and police were ordered; the tour was canceled; personal calls were made by Vernon to fan club presidents asking that they not attend; clothing was chosen; songs were chosen; ministers were contacted; the procession was planned — and the body was put on private display by 11:30 the next morning.

To the shocked world Elvis was dead, but apparently just four months after his death he was caught in a photograph sitting in his favorite chair overlooking the throngs of admirers visiting his grave. Elvis might not have even needed an escape by helicopter, because in 1968 a tunnel entrance was found on the grounds of Graceland that dates back to the Civil War and the Underground Railroad. More than 300 feet long, the tunnel exits the Graceland property's southeastern corner. Did Elvis ever use it? In just a few short years after his death, a rash of Elvis mania proclaiming 'He Lives!' would take on a life of its own, prompting investigative reports from ABC and best-selling books by authors seeking to prove that Elvis never died.

Elvis in DEA jogging suit (The Presley Assignment)

5.
Elvis Lives!

Hello like before
I'd never come here
If I'd known that you were here
I must admit though
That's it's nice to see you, dear
You look like you've been doing well
Hello like before
I hope we've grown
'Cause we were only children then
For laughs I guess we both can say
'I knew YOU when'
But then again, that's kiss and tell
Hello like before
I guess it's different
'Cause we know each other now
I guess I've always known
We'd meet again somehow
So then it might as well be now

—Bill Withers

Enter by the narrow gate. For the gate is wide and the way is easy that leads to destruction, and those who enter by it are many. For the gate is narrow and the way is hard that leads to life, and those who find it are few. — Matthew 7:13

The first time that I appeared on stage, it scared me to death. I really didn't know what all the yelling was about. I didn't realize that my body was moving. It's a natural thing to me. So to the manager backstage I said, "What'd I do? What'd I do?" And he said "Whatever it is, go back and do it again." — Elvis

The Colonel Tom Parker had created a new identity for himself after coming to America as an illegal Dutch immigrant, and if there was one man who could assist in giving Elvis a second life, it was him. In addition, Elvis had strong ties with the government; as FBI documents later revealed, he went by the alias John Burrows when he traveled. There's a popular rumor that Elvis flew to Argentina after the funeral; this of course is only hearsay and can't be verified. Many believe Elvis couldn't have given up performing cold turkey, and that the desire to perform would grow once his life in exile became a bore. The story of Orion supports the theory that Elvis attempted an incognito comeback.

Shortly after the King's death, a masked singer by the name of Orion emerged on the scene. He looked and he sang just like Elvis, but because of the mask, no one could tell his identity. This led to wild rumors that Elvis was back. Fans claimed that Orion left the stage between songs, and appeared to have body doubles filling in for him throughout his performances. The original Orion would get rather sweaty fast, and wouldn't last but a few songs before disappearing backstage, only to be replaced by a fresher, slimmer Orion. One fan described how she rushed into a tour bus at an Orion show only to see two Orions in the back of the bus. She claimed that one ducked into the bathroom before she could get a good look at him, but he appeared to look like Elvis. However, Orion was just the poor ol'country singer Jimmy Ellis, a man who happened to sound and look like Elvis. Ironically Ellis was also a poor boy from Mississippi with a mother named Gladys. He lived a rough-and-tumble life that ended in 1998 when he was murdered in his pawn shop in Alabama. Orion recently resurfaced in a 2014 comedic segment on *The Tonight Show* hosted by Jimmy Fallon. Fallon played the song "Washing Machine" and, when not laughing, couldn't help notice how much Orion sounded like Elvis. Orion was definitely not Elvis.

Making the case even more twisted is the fictional story called *Orion* written by Gail Brewer-Giorgio about a legendary singer who wanted to escape being famous by faking his own death.

Brewer-Giorgio, an aspiring writer from Atlanta, submitted her story to the William Morris Agency for publication after Elvis' death and before the real Orion ever performed. Without knowing it, Brewer-Giorgio wrote of events in *Orion* that had actually taken place in Elvis Presley's life. It was a case of life imitating art. Or was it?

In 1979, the ABC television show 20/20 did an investigation into the circumstances surrounding the alleged death of Elvis Presley as the public's fascination peaked with the 'Elvis Lives!' fever drummed up by Brewer-Giorgio's book. The investigative report ironically supported the case for Elvis faking his death. With the cat possibly out of the bag *Orion* disappeared from bookstores across the country. Supposedly, *Orion*, Brewer-Giorgio's first book netted her a $75,000 advance, but after the book disappeared she feared it wouldn't make enough to cover the advance, leaving her with little financial gain. So Brewer-Giorgio drummed up more 'Elvis Lives!' hysteria with the release of a series of Elvis-is-alive themed books and a cassette tape, claiming to have recorded an Elvis phone conversation in 1986. But the reason the voice on the tape does a good impersonation of the King is that it is him. It has been proved to be a spliced set of answers to questions edited into a monologue from a real Elvis interview from 1962. Fans should check out the "Elvis Aron Presley" box set for the monologue, and "Golden Celebration" for the interview.

Once the "evidence" in Brewer-Giorgio's second book *Is Elvis Alive* goes out the window, there is very little else to take seriously, as the book basically becomes a plug for the *Orion* novel. If Elvis really didn't die in 1977, he probably died laughing when he read this book, which is full of the author's supposed psychic abilities, astrological mumbo jumbo and government conspiracies. When her novel got pulled off the shelves Brewer-Giorgio believed it was for coming too close to the truth, but in fact it was a clever marketing ploy that not only kept Elvis in the spotlight, but put her in a position to sell millions of copies.

Girls, Girls, Girls Poster (Paramount)

A problem when examining the death of Elvis is that he was loved by so many people, and they will look for and find anomalies that make them believe Elvis is indeed alive. There are plenty of weird things to cling to, and one is the existence of a dude called Jesse, who at 70 years old looks like an aged Elvis. He even exhibits similar bone and facial structures in the only picture that we have of him, released in a book published in 2001. A Tennessee doctor alleged he had been treating Jesse (Elvis) for

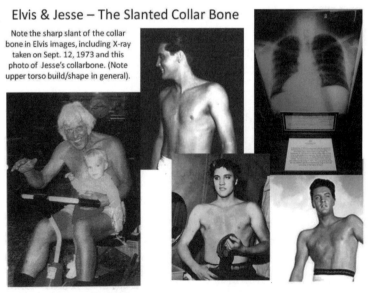

Elvis as Jesse? (Lindahoodsigmontruth.com)

Elvis is not Jesse (The Presley Assignment)

years, and the picture was snapped when Lisa Marie took her son to see his grandfather.

But Mickey Moran from The Presley Assignment discredits the shady photo, and outs its champion, Linda Hood Sigmon, as a sincere believer easily fooled. Moran writes:

> In the summer of 1997, Dr. Hinton began treating Jesse for chronic pain. Dr. Hinton tells in his book that he saw what Jesse looked like for the first time in November 1997. This tells us that Dr. Hinton was treating Jesse without ever meeting him. Linda Hood Sigmon showed Dr. Hinton the picture of Jesse sitting on the riding lawn mower. Dr. Hinton never saw Jesse in person before or after treating him. Linda asked Dr. Hinton to treat "Elvis" over the phone for chronic pain but the prescriptions were all made out to her. Of course, this was illegal on Dr. Hinton's part. Hinton claimed once that he saw Elvis "eye to eye" but that was a play on words because he saw the eyes of Jesse in the photo. It is documented in Hinton's own book that he had not examined or met Jesse in person before or after treatment. Linda had been tricked into all of this by con men looking to score some drugs. The con men were Joel Tim Zophy and Terry Campbell. Tim Zophy was convicted in 1993 for racketeering, extortion, and for sending threatening communications. Linda's Jesse photograph was taken at the campgrounds

in Moneta, VA. It is believed to be Tim Zophy's camper in the background. Mr. Zophy had circulated the photo before and claimed that it was Elvis with his son, LeRoy, by a woman named Nancy. He told people that Elvis refused to financially support the child and had asked for donations to help raise the child. Tim said Nancy was raising the child as a lone parent because Elvis had AIDS. After that, the photo recycled and turned up in Hinton's book as Elvis with his grandson, Benjamin, and is the photo that Linda tries to pass off as Elvis. If you look at the photo above you will see what "Jesse" looked like in 1950. These two photos are obviously of the same person and is NOT [sic] Elvis. [14]

Unfortunately there are no other images to go on, and the whole story comes from an obscure self-published book *The Truth about Elvis Aron Presley: In His Own Words* released in 2001. The book, written by Dr. Donald Hinton and his mysterious co-author Jesse, claims that Jesse was actually an older Elvis who faked his death with the help of Colonel Tom Parker. As noted by Moran above, the poor Dr. Hinton who wrote the book never actually met "Jesse," and was duped into writing hundreds of prescriptions for high dosage painkillers. Author and probate attorney Andrew W. Mayoras writes:

> According to Dr. Hinton, Jesse had to get away from the life of Elvis for several reasons, primarily because of his poor health and due to threats against him and his family. Col. Parker agreed to help because he could earn lots of money from doing so, Dr. Hinton said. Indeed, Elvis has been at or near the top of Forbes' list of the highest earning dead celebrities for years. Dr. Hinton said he treated Jesse for nearly six years for pain management due to his arthritic condition and other medical problems. He claimed that Jesse opened up to him and told him of his true identity. His book included many handwritten letters by Jesse and said it was Jesse's way of re-introducing

himself to the world. There were a few problems with Dr. Hinton's story. One was that he promised in the book that Elvis/Jesse would reveal himself to the world in 2002. Obviously, that never happened. Another was that the book led to an investigation of Dr. Hinton for mail fraud, by the Missouri Attorney General's office, as well as by the DEA and Missouri Healing Arts Board for illegally prescribing medications to Jesse.

Dr. Hinton actually lost his ability to prescribe medicine and was placed on five months' probation by the medical board. But the Dr. Hinton investigation did lead to an interesting place. When Dr. Hinton came under attack, his patient, Jesse, wrote a letter to the Attorney General supporting Dr. Hinton and refuting the mail fraud claims. He included the following in his letter, "Sir, I don't know if you believe in my continued existence or not, but if I continue to expose myself like I did in the book, I will be eliminated very easily. Pure and simple as that." The Attorney General's office had the letter analyzed by a special type of handwriting expert, Shirley Mason, who was a certified graphologist. Graphology is commonly used by the FBI and throughout Europe, but is not universally accepted. Mason worked for the Kansas City Bureau of Investigation for many years, successfully using graphology as evidence in criminal court cases. Shirley Mason reported that she compared the Jesse letter to past letters written by Elvis. So what did she have to say about it?

Not only did they match, Mason wrote, but she would testify in court, under oath, that Elvis "has to be ALIVE." She felt the handwriting was "UNMISTAKABLE." The Attorney General's office cleared Dr. Hinton of all charges. A television reporter in Cleveland, Suzanne Stratford, began investigating. She interviewed Dr. Hinton on camera and analyzed the evidence, including the Mason report, a picture taken six months after the funeral of what looked like Elvis peering through a screen door (and certified by Kodak), and the fact that Elvis' tombstone lists his middle name as "Aaron" when official records show his true middle name to be "Aron." Stratford also reported that Dr. Hinton had passed a lie detector test they had administered. And there's more! Stratford reported she was contacted by Jesse. She asked for, and received, a sample of Jesse's DNA in 2002, so it could be tested. Fox 8 News did in fact test the DNA sample against known "control" samples of Elvis, including a 1975 liver biopsy sample and tissue from his autopsy. The problem was that they didn't match. But again, another interesting turn. Not only did the "Jesse" sample not match the other two samples—they didn't match each other. In other words, Elvis' autopsy tissue did not match the liver tissue from 1975.

So where did the autopsy sample come from? Does this mean that Elvis' autopsy was faked? Maybe. But, of course, there's only one person alive (other than Jesse, of course) who can definitively prove or disprove whether Jesse is Elvis—Elvis' daughter. Fox 8 News contacted Lisa Marie Presley's representatives and asked for a sample of her DNA to find out the truth. She declined. [15]

However, the strange story that Jesse was actually Elvis falls apart rather quickly according to molecular biologist Terri Sundquist, who after listening to a lecture by Anthony Tambasco about DNA and Elvis conspiracies at the 20th International Symposium on Human Identification in Las Vegas, wrote:

> The story starts with a doctor's claim that he is treating Elvis Presley, who assumed the identity of his twin brother Jesse Presley after faking his death. To determine whether Elvis Presley is still alive and using his brother's name, investigators contacted "Jesse" and performed a number of tests. Handwriting samples

provided by "Jesse" were compared to letters written by Elvis, but these comparisons yielded inconclusive results. Fingerprint cards from Elvis Presley and "Jesse" did not match. DNA testing was also performed. However, finding a suitable reference sample to generate Elvis Presley's DNA profile proved challenging. Materials submitted as reference samples included a scarf, which yielded degraded DNA and thus no suitable profile, a blood-stained pair of jeans, which yielded a mixture of male and female DNA, and tissue samples taken during two liver biopsies and Elvis's autopsy, which yielded DNA profiles that did not match each other. None of these profiles matched that of "Jesse." To complicate matters even more, a woman named Eliza then surfaces, claiming to be Elvis's half-sister. She underwent DNA testing, and the results were consistent with her being a half-sister to "Jesse" and related to a paternal first cousin, but not a maternal first cousin, of Elvis. Thus, her DNA results could not disprove the hypotheses that she is Elvis's half-sister and "Jesse" is really Elvis living under a different name. However, as Tambasco phrased it in an interview with the media, "many unrelated people can exhibit similar DNA markers." [16]

If Elvis didn't die, neither did his myth, which seems to have its own force of regenerating energy. Of course if he were around today, he would be over 70 and it's hard to say whether his career would have been able to carry on like it has. Like dead pop stars Jim Morrison, James Dean and others whose fame solely depends upon their youthful sex appeal dying relatively young made it possible for Elvis to continue selling records and influencing different generations while raking in a fortune for his estate. The Elvis-is-alive legend transcends those of his pop culture contemporaries. Elvis' magnetic persona and the effect he had on the lives of baby boomers created the need to keep him alive. If Elvis died, then so did the defining icon of an entire generation. The most believable reason for the 'Elvis Lives!' mythos has nothing to do with 'facts.'

He simply was the greatest entertainer of his generation, and his fans crave the reassurance of his company, even if it has to come from beyond the grave, a cold netherworld where the legend inside the casket might not have faked his death but been actually murdered.

6.
Elvis versus the Mafia

Well listen to me, you young hoods, this is some advice
You do the crime, you're payin the price
Cause if you're in the drug spots, sellin crack on the block
Snatchin chains, bustin brains, like a real hardrock
If you ever hear a cop say you're under arrest
Go out just like a trooper, stick out your chest
Cause you might have been robbin, you might have been whylin
But you won't be smilin on Riker's Island
Just to hear the name it makes your spine tingle
This is a jungle where the murderers mingle
This ain't a place that's crowded but there's room for you
Whether you're white or you're black, you'll be black and blue
Cause in every cellblock, there is a hardrock
with a real nice device that's called a sock lock
Don't ever get caught in a crime my friend
Cause this bus trip is not to Adventure's Inn
They have a nice warm welcome, for new inmates
Razors, and shanks, and sharp edged plates
Posses will devour, punks with power
After the shower it's, rush hour
So watch your back before you get sacked
These a bunch of maniacs that's about to attack
If you're a hustlin pro, keep a low profile'n
Cause you won't be smilin on Riker's Island
—Kool G Rap

Do not be deceived: Bad company ruins good morals.
— 1 Corinthians 15:33

The image is one thing and the human being is another... it's
very hard to live up to an image. — Elvis

79

Moving on to the curious reports that Elvis was secretly working with the Feds and that they had a hand in putting him in the witness protection program, making it easy for him to drop off the grid...

It is no secret Elvis had a fascination with government, police work, and the law. He was named an honorary sheriff in many towns and even met with then President Nixon to discuss how he could be used to spy on various groups, including the Black Panthers and the Mafia in an effort to help the government. What we know of Elvis' beginnings show he was a naïve, honest young man, and it is possible that this boyish innocence could have played right into questionable hands. After all, he was in the military and would have been a perfect candidate on which to try out MK-ULTRA techniques. Eventually however, even an unsophisticated, simple man who searches will find certain Truths. A searcher is someone who constantly grows both in knowledge, and in inner strength. Could the joke have been on us?

Around 1977, Elvis was facing a low point in his life—sick of being famous and all it entailed for him, including a very public separation and divorce from Priscilla after she left him for karate instructor Mike Stone. The King hadn't made the cut as a dreamy, fairy-tale husband and his parade of younger beauty contestant girlfriends was losing its appeal thanks to his depleted sex drive. If he wanted to fake his own death as a way out of the public eye, he definitely had the money and connections to pull it off. It's interesting to note that a few of his prized possessions, including a family Bible, several pharmaceutical books, *Cheiro's Book of Numbers*, the book *Autobiography of a Yogi*, extensive amounts of jewelry, pictures of his mother and his private plane, along with over a million dollars from a private checking account all disappeared and were never recovered after his death. Mickey Moran writes on his website The Presley Assignment:

> Phone records show that Ginger Alden, Elvis' girlfriend at the time of his alleged death, phoned the *National Enquirer* one to three hours before calling downstairs for help when she found Elvis on the bathroom

floor. How did she know to call them one to three hours before there was anything to call about? Did she know that there was going to be a body in there later on? Dee Presley, Elvis' stepmother, said she received a call from someone that sounded like [Elvis] and saying things only Elvis knew. Elvis' father refused to have his son's coffin draped with the American flag, traditionally given to all dead veterans. Did he know that the coffin did not contain his son's body? Elvis was extremely vain and obsessed with his personal image; his hair if he had not dyed it repeatedly would have been completely silver and he was embarrassed about his recent weight gain. In the months before his so-called death Elvis gained over 50 pounds in three months and weighed nearly 275 pounds even though his death certificate lists him at an active 170 pounds. The original death certificate vanished, and the current death certificate is dated two months after his alleged death.[17]

The FBI recently declassified the secret files they had been keeping on Elvis since the '60s, however more than 80% of the files are dated from August 1977 and after. What did they know? Some believe Elvis was working with the FBI to expose and take down organized crime rings. According to rumors, Elvis had been tapped by the FBI to help infiltrate 'the fraternity' a crew with strong ties to the Mafia. By August 1977 the FBI thought they had enough evidence to bring the mob to justice. On August 15th Elvis met with his lawyers and federal agents in downtown Memphis to prep for the next day's courthouse appearance, where Elvis would testify before a grand jury. Elvis would be dead less than 24 hours later. It would be interesting to know what was actually said during this meeting. Maybe it was a high level black ops meeting discussing his "death"? Or, did the Mafia simply get to him before he could testify? It is possible Elvis' life was in danger and he knew it, and so would have the FBI.

Elvis as Lawman began in December 1970 with his induction into the Drug Enforcement Agency (DEA) by President Nixon.

Elvis had just been named one of America's Ten Outstanding Young Men for his efforts to wipe out drugs, even though Elvis was a serious drug addict. He went undercover for the DEA in 'Operation Fountain Pen' and vowed to take down the criminal underworld. Six years before his "death" Elvis was given a tour of FBI facilities and presented with a CNOA Membership Certificate certifying that Elvis was a member in good standing of the California Narcotics Officers Association. Elvis even pulled out the certificate once on stage, trying to prove to the audience he wasn't strung out on dope like the gossip rags claimed. He told the audience, "This is from the International Narcotics Enforcement Association. This Certificate gives me special honors and a lifelong membership. I've been wearing a federal narcotics badge for six years. They don't give you that if you're strung out." But Elvis was beyond strung out, his body was a living pharmacy.

When Elvis wasn't reading about pills, he was studying religion, history and metaphysics. One of his favorite books, displayed now at Graceland, was *The Passover Plot* by Hugh Schonfield published in 1966. The book is a story of how Jesus may have faked his death and returned years later instead of being resurrected. But according to an explosive new report by the *National Enquirer,* the King didn't fake the funk, but instead was murdered by the Mafia in one of the slickest whacks ever.

That Elvis had ties to the Mafia is undisputed. In one instance, underworld ring leader Fred Pro and a co-conspirator, Phil Kitzer, devised a plan to buy Elvis' plane, refurbish it and lease it back to the Presleys. Fred Pro was going to lease the aircraft out again for tax purposes, and have Elvis receive profits. As the undercover operation was staged, the FBI files show that Fred Pro took out a $1 million loan against the plane and left the bank stuck holding the aircraft. It was at this point that the FBI came in and arrested Fred Pro, Phil Kitzer, and their associates. It is possible that after this, Elvis received threats from the crime world, as it was around this time that Elvis started wearing bulletproof vests. He became so paranoid that, according to some Graceland insiders, Elvis wore

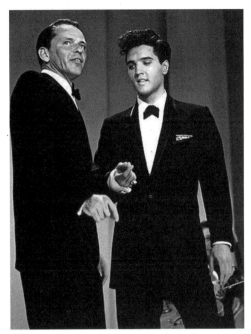

Elvis with Frank Sinatra (Getty Images)

the protective gear even inside his home. As the '70s dawned, the mob's rule over Vegas was in serious jeopardy. The *National Enquirer* explains:

> In 1969 the Corporate Gaming Act, which curtailed the influence of organized crime, was passed in Las Vegas. The act made it possible for corporations to own casinos and Elvis, because of his interaction in Las Vegas, was obviously privy to first-hand information and it was even speculated that the King knew what had happened to Jimmy Hoffa of the Teamsters Union, who had used the union's pension funds to invest in the construction of hotels, including Ceasar's Palace, and Circus Circus, owned or constructed by Moe Dalitz. Elvis met Dalitz, who was the Vegas man for Chicago crime boss, Sam Giancana, sometime in the 1950s and Dalitz was often seen on Elvis' film sets. Elvis was most likely telling the FBI everything he knew or heard about the mob's activities in Vegas and when Jimmy Hoffa vanished, the

gangsters were afraid Elvis—who had now joined the Fed's sting operation "Fountain Pen"—had information that could put them away. Elvis was jeopardizing a multi-billion dollar enterprise for the mob because even if his information wasn't solid enough to bury the mob, the impact of Elvis testifying at their trials would destroy them in court and inside mob tipsters have revealed that after much deliberation, the crime bosses determined Elvis had to go and conveniently, Elvis died shortly before he was set to testify. [18]

Years later, actress Suzanna Leigh, who co-starred with Presley in the flick *Paradise Hawaiian Style,* claimed in her memoir that Elvis' father Vernon always believed his son was murdered, a theory shared by ex-detective and head of Elvis' security team, Dick Grob. The *National Enquirer* continues:

, Elvis had too much information on the Vegas crime lords to be allowed to live and his killer, who had to have been a professional hit man, along with someone inside Elvis' immediate circle at Graceland had to be involved in the murder. The mission would have required only for the murderer to gain access to Graceland. Obviously armed with information about the entertainer's deadly prescription pill habit, it would have been easy to commit the crime within a 24-hour period by sneaking into a medicine cabinet—or wherever Elvis kept his arsenal of pain killers—and switch them for something stronger that would make the crime look like [a] self-inflicted overdose. Interrogators who were called in after his death was reported actually believed this is what had happened.

Even the King himself knew he had a serious allergy to codeine pain killers, yet autopsy revealed his body contained ten times the normal dosage of the drug at the time of death. An investigator into the crime was quoted as saying, "In fact, everything about the case points to Elvis being murdered in this manner."

Today it is no secret Elvis was battling an addiction to

prescription medications. However, in preparation for the role he was about to play as a star witness, he was working on kicking the habit. It was revealed after his death that Elvis had 14 different drugs in his system when he died, but none of the dosages were found in lethal levels except for the amount of codeine, which, according to Dr. Eric Muirhead, a pathologist who assisted with the autopsy, "was off the charts!" It makes no sense that Elvis, who was aware of his allergy to this particular drug, would have intentionally taken this drug, particularly in an amount that would have put even someone without a deadly allergy to it in the morgue. This indicates that the drug was the murder weapon, since it is a drug Elvis would have never have knowingly used because of his allergy. There were several statements made by investigators to this effect, including this one: "There was a switch! Elvis took the painkiller Dilaudid along with his cocktail of prescription drugs to help combat his rampant insomnia. The killer only had to switch codeine tablets into pill bottles marked Dilaudid."

Putting together pieces of information found in FBI files, toxicology reports, pathology reports, court documents, and

Elvis with Ann Margaret in Viva Las Vegas (Paramount)

statements from Elvis' close associates, the evidence points to a killer who had intimate knowledge of the King's secret pill habit and used this information to stage a murder that would look like a death from natural causes, or at the most, an accidental overdose. "Drug overdoses have long been a good cover for celebrity deaths," said an organized crime source. "Everybody in the Vegas underworld knew Elvis took pills. It was his weakness, and it was only natural for the killer to exploit that weakness." [18]

If a mob assassin was able to gain entrance to Graceland via a Judas in Elvis' inner circle, it wouldn't be difficult for him to switch the bottle of Dilaudid Elvis was given at 4 a.m. on the day of his death with a lethal dose of codeine. Knowing that Elvis couldn't sleep at night, and for the most part was a walking zombie, the killer could have switched Elvis' pills at any point when the singer wasn't in his bathroom. Elvis was addicted to Dilaudid and popped them religiously as part of his nightly sleep cocktail, however his newly acquired bottle of pills was found untouched in his bathroom after he died. Police have never explained where the other missing drugs from Elvis' bathroom went, and why the carpets were cleaned to remove the entertainer's vomit and by whom. One thing's for certain, Elvis was allergic to codeine and would never have taken the drug knowingly. His nurse, Marian Cocke, and former flame Linda Thompson both told investigators he'd react to the drug by breaking out in rashes, experiencing breathing problems and panic attacks. Besides, who needs codeine when you have the much more kick-ass Dilaudid laying around? Yet Elvis was pumped with more than 500 milligrams of codeine only a few hours before he died. Combined with the other drugs already swimming in his system, the added codeine would have been a significant factor in the cause of his death. If Elvis did "die" it was because of anaphylactic shock, caused by extreme allergic reactions inducing swelling in the throat, pulmonary congestion and edema. Death by anaphylactic shock would be beneficial to the mob, since it is hard to trace in a postmortem procedure. The King's "death" has been attributed by various medical experts and pundits to a huge range of causes: heart attack, drug overdose, head trauma, autoimmune disorders and even a case of the killer constipation.

Whether Elvis was murdered or his death was a hoax, the concept of meeting the maker weighed heavily on his mind during the final year of his life. Underlined in one of his favorite books was the sentence, "If I should return you would not recognize me." Dying, or the ability to leave your material possessions behind and become a new person, was a reoccurring theme Elvis frequently spoke about before vanishing. His spiritual beliefs and philosophies were just as complex as the man himself. Although rooted in deep Southern Christianity Elvis was a seeker of occult knowledge and esoteric spirituality. He was fascinated with numbers, and might have left clues behind in one of his favorite books detailing how he was going to fake his own death.

Elvis at the L.A. Forum 1970 (*L.A. Times*)

Elvis at the L.A. Forum 1970 (*L.A. Times*)

Elvis at the L.A. Forum 1970 (*L.A. Times*)

Elvis is Alive: The Complete Conspiracy

7.
Elvis the Esoteric

I think about a world to come
Where the books were found
by the Golden ones
Written in pain, written in awe
By a puzzled man who questioned
What we were here for
All the strangers came today
And it looks as though
they're here to stay
— David Bowie

Love is patient and kind; love does not envy or boast; it is not
arrogant or rude. It does not insist on its own way; it is not
irritable or resentful; it does not rejoice at wrongdoing, but
rejoices with the truth. Love bears all things, believes all things,
hopes all things, endures all things. Love never ends. As for
prophecies, they will pass away; as for tongues, they will cease;
as for knowledge, it will pass away.
— Corinthians 13:4-8

Truth is like the sun. You can shut it out for a time,
but it ain't goin' away.
— Elvis

Elvis was fascinated with numerology, an interest fed by reading
an assortment of material on the subject. His particular favorite
was *Cheiro's Book of Numbers*. Elvis probed into numerology
so much that he became obsessed with it. He pondered over why
the number seven shows up so frequently in religious symbolism,
and became fascinated by the University founded by the ancient
Greek philosopher Pythagoras that dealt with sacred geometry
and esoteric mathematics. Now understanding that math was

91

the language of the universe, Elvis referred to *Cheiro's Book of Numbers* frequently. John Lennon also fixated on the *Book of Numbers* and wouldn't do anything without checking it first. Robert Rosen, author of *The Final Days of John Lennon* writes:

> After Lennon discovered this book, which explained in simple language the occult "science" of numerology, he couldn't so much as dial a phone number without first consulting Cheiro, and he couldn't walk out of the house without finding mystical significance in every license plate, address, and street sign. Lennon, who was born on October 9, had always been aware of the strong presence of the number 9 in his life. He considered it his lucky number. His son Sean was also born on October 9; he'd written songs titled *Revolution 9*, *One After 909*, and *No. 9 Dream*; Brian Epstein first saw the Beatles at The Cavern on November 9; and he met Yoko on November 9. But it was only after reading Cheiro that Lennon came to understand that the multiples of 9, particularly 18 and 27, were as important as 9 itself. As Cheiro explained, the single numbers 1 to 9 represent "the physical or material side of things" and compound numbers from 10 on represent the "occult or spiritual side of life." Lennon spent a great deal of time making notes on the "birth numbers" and calculating, according to Cheiro's arcane formula, the "name numbers" of those closest to him. There were 9's and 18's everywhere. Yoko Ono was born February 18. Paul McCartney was born June 18. John equals 18 or 9. (According to Cheiro's laws, all compound numbers should be reduced to a single number.) Yoko Ono equals 9. Sean Ono Lennon equals 9. Paul equals 9. Richard Starkey (Ringo's real name) equals 9. Mimi Smith (the aunt who raised him) equals 9. The Dakota, on West 72nd Street (9), was built in 1881, which equals 18 or 9. And the year, 1980, was also an 18 or 9. [19]

Numbers and the supposed significance they held consumed

both Lennon and Elvis during the final months of their lives. The little book written by the mysteriously named Chiero was like a bible to them. But who was Cheiro? And could his work truly be taken seriously? Cheiro was the pen name of an Irishman born William Warner in 1866. He grew to be a roaming mystic claiming to have learned the ancient secrets of palmistry while living in India. After returning to Europe in the 1890s, Chiero became a notable palmist and mystic, telling the fortunes of several celebrities like Mata Hari, Oscar Wilde, Thomas Edison, and Mark Twain. He correctly told a then broke Twain that he would come into money in six years, and warned Wilde that if he didn't change his ways he would end up in a jail cell in seven. Oscar wound up in jail and Mark Twain signed an unexpectedly lush deal with Harper. Cheiro was an expert in palmistry but also wrote more than a dozen books on astrology and Chaldean numerology, including his most famous work, *Cheiro's Book of Numbers,* first published in 1926.

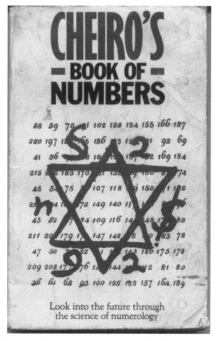

Chiero's Book of Numbers (Robert Rosen)

The book chronicled how numbers could be used to describe a person's character and ultimate fate based on their name, birthday and astrological chart. According to Cheiro's theory, Elvis was an eight, and based on the characteristics of "eights" he seemed a perfect fit. These individuals are misunderstood and lonely on the inside, despite being showered with love on the outside. They are deep thinkers and in tune with nature, but also rebellious and eccentric. Elvis shared being an "eight" with the Colonel and figured that might be the reason they were able to remain in business together for so long. He also loved that his two favorite actors, James Dean and Peter Sellers, were also eights.

Elvis further explored the significance of the numbers seven, three and nine, all of which are important esoteric mathematical keys to understanding how Elvis might have faked his death. Elvis disappeared on August 16, 1977. When you add those numbers together (8+16+1977) you get 2001. The movie *2001* was Elvis' favorite, and he used its eerie theme as his concert-opening theme

A team of astronauts are about to descend into a lunar excavation to take a look at the mysterious monolith.

MGM Presents "**2001: A SPACE ODYSSEY**" Super Panavision
A Stanley Kubrick Production and METROCOLOR®

2001 Lobby Card (MGM)

94

song. Considering that *2001* is the greatest esoteric film ever made, it's no wonder Elvis loved it so much. Because he was a good Christian boy at heart, Elvis was extremely fascinated with the trinity and sets of three, e.g., Father, Son, and Holy Ghost. The sum of the digits in the name of his favorite film (*2001*) is three (2+0+0+1). 2001 (favorite film) less 1977 (year of death) is 24. The two numbers from the day of death (8 and16) when added up equal 24. That is his age backwards (he was 42). The sum of the digits in the year of death (1+9+7+7) also equals 24. That is three occurrences of the number 24, which is divisible by three, and when divided by three the result is Elvis' primo number, eight. Eight also has a perfect cubed root (2x2x2=8). Elvis loved numerology, and when you consider the numeric significance of the date of his alleged death, it is clear that if indeed he did plan to fake his death, he could not have chosen a better date. Look into the presence of his number eight in the date 8-16-1977. Of course, the month of August being the eighth month is obvious to everyone, but we have 1×8, 2×8, 3×8 which equals 8, 16, and 24. So, there we have multiplications of 888 as well as 8+8+8=24. So this alone was an amazing date for Elvis, and if we add 24 back to 1977, we again get 2001! So, not only did August 16, 1977 produce 2001 by two different methods as shown above, it was loaded with the numbers 8, 24, 42, and 2001. To recap, adding the digits of 1977 produces 24, and 24 added to 1977 equals 2001. And get this: 1956 was the year in which Elvis burst upon the scene, 1+9+5+6=21, and 21+1956=1977!

Elvis with Larry Geller in Hawaii 1977 (Larry Geller)

While Elvis was getting deeper into numerology and occult studies, the Colonel and his boys hoped it would be a quickly passing fad. They resented Larry Geller for introducing Elvis to this new utopia of knowledge. Geller was Elvis' personal hairdresser and spiritual guru; as a teenager he even saw the King perform at the Pan Pacific Auditorium in Los Angeles. In his twenties Geller became the *go to* hairdresser in Hollywood, styling the likes of Peter Sellers, Sam Cooke, and Steve McQueen. Geller recalls (reprinted as found on the website elvisinfonet.com):

I was only 24 yet it was no big deal if we went over to Frank Sinatra's house for instance! But the thought of meeting Elvis, that was 'over-the-top' for me. He was The Man, he was The King, he was a legend! So I drove up to Bel-Air & the Perugia Way house and you could tell which one it was because there were tons of people outside! As I drove through the gates, girls were screaming, "Tell Elvis I'm here & Tell Elvis I Love him" and I'm thinking "Wow, this is something else!" I went into the house and Elvis walks up to me and says, *"Hi, I'm Elvis Presley"* and I put my hand out and say, 'Hi, I'm Larry Geller.' Elvis was about 5ft 11½ tall and I'm 6ft 2 and I have this deja-vu of 8 years earlier when I was the kid looking up at this same man when I saw him in the car park. I shook his hand and he says, *"Let's go into the bathroom, you can do my hair and we can talk."*

We walk into his bathroom and I expected to see all the Hollywood trappings of salon chairs and everything else but there's nothing! Elvis says *"C'mon man, we'll do it right here"* and just puts his head in the basin! I start to shampoo his hair and as I'm rinsing the suds off his hair he rears his head up and starts shaking. Water is flying & splattering everywhere, over me, over him. He looks at me with that Elvis smile, that grin, and he says. *"Hey man, what the hell! At least it's clean!"* When he said that I thought what a down to earth guy Elvis was. I just knew right away that he was real, he wasn't fake. It took about 45 minutes to finish his hair and the whole time Elvis didn't say a word, but his eyes would follow every move I made. I was working with people like Warren Beatty & Paul Newman and the most handsome guys of the movies but I can tell you no one looked like Elvis Presley. Elvis eclipsed them all! He had the face, the voice, the career, the fans, the fame, the money and he had the hair! His hair was unbelievable to work on. Once I'd finished and sprayed it I asked him, "So, what do you think Elvis?" Elvis looks and says, *"Yeah, yeah great but I want to ask you a question Larry. What are you really in to? What are you really all about?"* I thought to myself, 'Wow, this guy didn't say a word and now he's getting really personal.'

So I tell him the truth about my interests and this was way before The Beatles explosion and the Maharishi stuff became popular. So I told him how I worked as a hairdresser as a living but that more importantly was my search for the truth, for the purpose of life, for God. I said, "I know you're Elvis Presley and the biggest star in the world and what I'm saying probably sounds very corny to you." But Elvis replies, *"No, wait a minute. Larry you have no idea how I need to hear what you have to say. Please keep on talking."*

So I tell him about my meditation, yoga, my spiritual books, being vegetarian and everything. Right away he wanted to know about the soul, Do we have a soul? Where do we come from? Do we survive this life? ... all these things just emerged into this conversation. Well before I know it, it is an hour later and Elvis is talking to me and I look in the mirror and he has tears rolling down his cheeks. He's talking about his Mother and how poor they were and how she slaved her life away. How they didn't have running water in the house, but a well out the back. He talked about his still-born brother Jesse and about growing up in the church. We got into some major, major stuff and we had been talking about 3 hours. All of a sudden there was a knock at the door and this is so ironic that I'll never forget it. One of the guys said, "Hey boss, you all right in there?" Elvis replies, *"Sure man, of course I'm all right. What the hell do you think is going to happen to me in my own bathroom?"* Of course that was where it all ended, so how ironic is that? [20]

Elvis with Larry Geller and Jo Smith in Hawaii 1977
(Larry Geller)

Some of the esoteric books Elvis loved were:

• *The Impersonal Life* by Joseph Benner — Besides the Bible, this was Elvis' favorite book; he bought and gave away hundreds of copies to fans and friends.

• *Autobiography of a Yogi* by Paramahansa Yogananda — Elvis was attracted to the idea of leaving your earthly possessions

Elvis with Ginger and Terry Alden in Hawaii 1977
(Ginger Alden)

behind, and he even joined the 'Self-Realization Fellowship' run by Daya Mata.

• *In Search of the Miraculous* by P. D. Ouspensky — A student of Gurdjieff, Ouspensky was a Russian philosopher who sought to prove the higher dimensions of existence and Transhumanist ideas with sacred geometry.

• *Freedom from the Known* by J. Krishnamurti — An Indian mystic who challenges us to find ourselves rather than relying on external authorities. Imagine Elvis reading this book while making a film like *Clambake*.

• *The Stranger* by Albert Camus — An existential novel about a good man who was sentenced to death, not so much for the crime he committed but because he was drastically different from the majority of people. Obviously, one of Elvis' all-time favorites.

• *Shambhala: Sacred Path of the Warrior* by Chogyam Trungpa — An excellent book that applies the principles of martial arts to everyday life. Elvis loved Martial Arts, was a fan of Bruce Lee and probably would have been a huge supporter of the UFC.

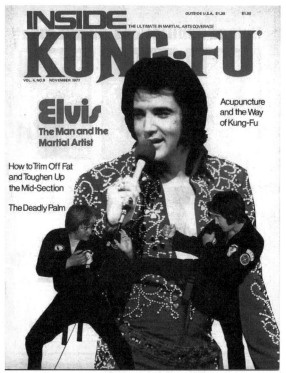

Elvis the Martial Artist (Inside Kung Fu)

• *The Prophet* by Kahlil Gibran — A classic thesis on the philosophy of love, life, death and marriage.

• *Life and Teaching of the Masters of the Far East* (a six volume set) by Baird T. Spalding — According to Spalding, "Mastership is bringing to the surface what is buried within by meditation and consulting with the Self." Elvis agreed.

Elvis acquired a collection of over 400 books on ancient myths and religions, metaphysics, self-help, spirituality, UFOs and the occult, which the Colonel saw as a threat. When Elvis discovered that Memphis Mafia foreman "Diamond" Joe Esposito was snitching to the Colonel about Elvis' spiritual activities, he promptly fired him. Priscilla was also drawn into his spiritual quest as she attended a handful of lectures by the great Masonic scholar Manly P. Hall. Elvis longed to go to the lectures but feared his presence would be too disruptive. She tried to be a good sport about it because she cared about Elvis, but after a while became fed up and finally told the King that she "found the lectures difficult to understand and painful to endure," much to his dismay. This spiritual rift, coupled with a non-existent sex life, eventually doomed their relationship.

Meanwhile, Elvis kept working. With every new movie, he was feeling increasing dissatisfaction, as they now all seemed to blur together, indistinguishable from one other. In the excellent book *The Seeker King: the Spiritual Biography of Elvis Presley,* Gary Tillery writes:

> During the filming of *Harum Scarum* Elvis was delving into *Autobiography of a Yogi*, which relates the life story of Mukunda Lal Ghosh, an Indian mystic who became famous under his religious name, Paramahansa Yogananda. Even as a boy Yogananda felt drawn to the spiritual life and searched for the proper guru. At seventeen he linked up with Swami Yukteswar Giri, a master of Kriya Yoga. The swami had amazing abilities, which he demonstrated for Yogananda over the years, including the power to materialize in more than one place at the same time. He himself had been initiated into Kriya Yoga in 1884 by Lahiri Mahasaya, a holy man who in 1861 had been tasked with reintroducing the ancient discipline to the world by an enigmatic figure Lahiri called Babaji. A simple accountant for the government, Lahiri had been out walking in the foothills of the Himalayas one day and had a "chance" encounter with Babaji. After speaking with him for a while, Lahiri had the odd feeling that he had known the reclusive figure before—and finally recognized him as his guru in previous incarnations. In time he would conclude that the mysterious Babaji was actually an avatar of Lord Krishna.

> After several days of instruction from Babaji, Lahiri returned to his home and devoted the rest of his life to the spread of Kriya Yoga. Unlike many holy men, he advised most of his disciples to continue their daily lives exactly

as before. For him, living in an enlightened state did not require renunciation of the world and being an ascetic. He made no distinction between Hindu, Muslim, Christian, or Jewish followers and was as welcoming to those of the lowest caste as he was a maharajah.

Yogananda became an adept at Kriya Yoga and traveled to the United States in 1920. He represented India that year at the International Congress of Religious Liberals. Except for a world tour in 1935–36, he remained in the U. S. for the rest of his life. He founded the Self-Realization Fellowship (SRF) in 1920 and established its headquarters in Los Angeles in 1925. He lectured widely and spread knowledge of Hindu beliefs and the benefits of Kriya Yoga wherever he went. In 1946 he published his autobiography, which included the stories of many holy men and the powers they displayed—amazing powers such as clairvoyance and levitation. Elvis was impressed by Yogananda's tales and also by the universalism of his approach. One day, on a break during the filming of *Harum Scarum*, he looked up from reading the book and informed Larry Geller that he thought he was ready for initiation into Kriya Yoga. To the stunned Geller, this was much like saying he thought now would be a good time for the Pope to name him a cardinal. Geller knew how demanding the training was because he had been through the two-year program himself. The first step was a yearlong regimen of daily physical exercises, health consciousness, and a stipulated schedule of meditation.

Nevertheless, Geller called the SRF headquarters in Los Angeles and made arrangements for Elvis to speak with its head, Sri Daya Mata. As Faye Wright, of Salt Lake City, she had become a disciple of Yogananda in 1931 and had worked closely with him until his death in 1952. She quickly agreed to meet with the King of Rock and Roll, and the next evening, after the day's filming, Elvis and Geller went to the SRF ashram

Elvis in Harum Scarum (MGM)

on Mount Washington. Elvis loved the sylvan setting, and he had an immediate rapport with Daya Mata. In her features and demeanor she reminded him of his mother. The more she described the aims of the Fellowship, the more excited he became. He said he was ready to turn his back on his career and join a monastery or start a commune. She advised him to go slow—that his development must be evolutionary. They discussed the process of training and meditation, and she gave him her personal lesson books to study. He accepted them gladly, but he had the unbridled enthusiasm of the novice. "This higher level of spirituality is what I've been seeking my whole life," he told her. "Now that I know where it is and how to achieve it, I want to teach it. I want to teach it to all my fans—to the whole world." Over the coming months he returned to the site often for solace. He read and meditated, but like most seekers he hoped for a short path to his goal, and it did not come. The cosmos did not care that he was Elvis Presley. [21]

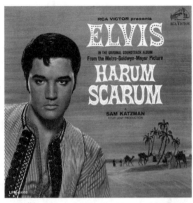

Harum Scarum album cover (RCA)

His spiritual quest continued as he began exploring the possibility of healing with his hands. Elvis focused on using the unseen energy that surrounds us, and was on more than one occasion able to demonstrate making bushes move using invisible forces beaming from his hands. He used his powers to help ease his grandmother's arthritis and stop Priscilla's headaches. Elvis believed that he could cure the flu and other ailments through his majestic touch. He was also convinced he could make leaves float, and turn the Bel Air Country Club's sprinklers on and off through telekinesis. Longtime Elvis bodyguard Sonny West, an initial skeptic, had an amazing encounter once with mystical Elvis. One day while Sonny's young son was sick, the King showed up at his house wearing a turban and asked to pray over the sick toddler. The baby had been suffering from a high fever, and Elvis was determined to heal the young child. He placed the baby on a green scarf and began chanting while moving his hands in circular motions. Although Sonny and his wife found the affair extremely strange, they were "amazed" to see the boy's temperature instantly go back to normal.

Perhaps Elvis' greatest spiritual feat took place on the side of a road somewhere near Nashville, when he saved an anonymous driver's life. The man, who moments earlier had pulled off the road while experiencing a heart attack, was now being rescued by the King of Rock 'n' Roll. Elvis pulled the man from the car and put one arm around his shoulder and placed the other on the stranger's heart. Moments later, the astonished stranger was perfectly fine. Tillery continues:

> As part of his spiritual training, Elvis liked to go outside in the middle of the night and spend hours watching the movement of the planets. He felt that there were waves of energy moving the planets through the universe and that with proper attunement they could be seen. One night he saw a UFO. He pointed it out to Sonny West, who at first thought it might be an airplane or helicopter. But the vehicle made no sound. They watched its approach through tree limbs as it passed over the house toward the front lawn. Elvis told Sonny to go get Jerry Schilling so he could see it, too. When the two came bounding out the front door, Elvis was nowhere to be seen. For a moment they worried that he had been abducted. Then they noticed him three doors away, staring toward the south, where the craft had disappeared. Geller gave Elvis a book about the subject. A week later, just after he had finished reading it, Elvis and some of the group were driving through New Mexico on Route 66. They saw a bright disk streaking across the dark sky, descending. Suddenly it stopped and made a right-angle turn, accelerating until it disappeared from view. Elvis said, "That was definitely not a shooting star or a meteor. It was clearly something different." Jerry Schilling commented, "We don't make anything that moves like that." Geller voiced what they were thinking, "That object maneuvered like a flying saucer." Still later, Elvis witnessed a UFO one evening at Graceland while in the company of his father. The eerie experience prompted Vernon to reminisce about the blue light he had seen the night Elvis was born in Tupelo. [21]

Elvis was curious to learn about the esoteric meaning of his own strange name, discovering that "El" traced back to ancient Hebrew and meant 'light' or 'shining one connected with God,' while "Vis" literally meant 'the power of God.' Elvis began

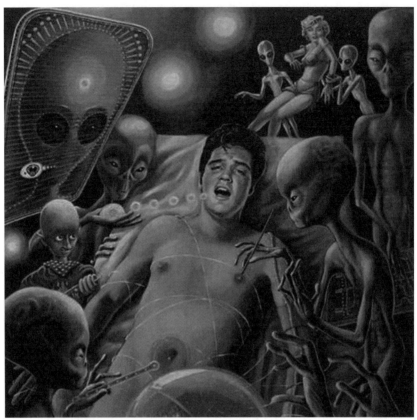

Elvis abducted by aliens (Beforeitsnews.com)

wearing a Jewish Chai pendant in addition to his cross and famously told a reporter when asked about it, "I don't want to be kept out of heaven on a technicality." He donated $12,500 to help build a Jewish community center in Memphis and added a Star of David to his mother's tombstone. Elvis was becoming a learned man and was anxious to share this newfound knowledge with everyone. He changed the spiritually-lost actress Deborah Wally's life after telling her, "Look we've only got this moment together, so let's have it completely. No holding back. No wasting time on trivialities. I've got the word; I want to give it you. I'm not a man. I'm not a woman—I'm a soul, a spirit, a force. I have no interest in anything of this world. I want to live in another dimension entirely."

By the summer of 1966 Elvis was back in a Nashville recording studio, cutting his first non-movie album in four years. He was in a spiritual mood and the landmark gospel album that he recorded, *How Great Thou Art,* reflects it. The late night sessions were electric and everyone in the studio knew something special was happening. After singing the title track "How Great Thou Art," Elvis seemed to glow like a ghost. Childhood friend Jerry Schilling watched in silent disbelief recalling, "When he got to the dramatic finish of the song, there was a strange hush in the room—nobody wanted to break the spell. I've been in a lot of recording studios since my time with Elvis, but I've never seen a performer undergo the kind of physical transition he did during that recording. He got to the end of the take and he was as white as a ghost, thoroughly exhausted, and in a kind of trance."

Elvis was sick of acting, and happy to be making music once again, charged up and re-energized from working with a new producer, Felton Jarvis. The pair shared an instant connection, and as the sessions progressed, Elvis ditched the initial material that he was supposed to be working on and dove headfirst into his beloved gospel collection. Elvis carefully combed through his records and chose a number of standards to record, with 11 backup singers to accompany him. Despite Jarvis officially being credited as producer, it's no secret that Elvis directed the recording sessions. Elvis was in the zone and ended up producing a solid twelve-song gospel album that would bring him his first Grammy Award, in 1967. In fact, Elvis won only three Grammy Awards during his astonishing music career and all three were for gospel recordings. With *How Great Thou Art,* Elvis truly created a spiritual musical masterpiece and possibly delivered the highlight of his recording career.

As Elvis' spiritual quest continued, he experimented with popular hippie practices like smoking weed and tripping on acid. He didn't like marijuana but found it harmless, except for the damage caused to the refrigerator. He had enough weight problems to worry about and didn't need the excess pounds that inevitably come with late night stoner munchies. Elvis' encounter with LSD was much more lucid:

> After reading Aldous Huxley's *The Doors of Perception* and Timothy Leary's *The Psychedelic Experience*, Elvis did try LSD—but just once. He first persuaded Red and Sonny West to try it in Los Angeles, with Larry Geller, Charlie Hodge, and himself watching the whole time to make sure they were safe. Then he and Priscilla tried it a few months later during his Christmas break at Graceland. They invited Geller, Lamar Fike, and Jerry Schilling to accompany them on their trip, while Sonny West was appointed to keep an eye on them. They started by sitting around a conference table in Elvis's upstairs office. After a while they saw each other's faces distorting and broke into laughter. Priscilla witnessed her husband's multicolored shirt grow larger and larger, spreading out so far that it seemed ready to burst. After about ninety minutes they stood up to stretch and realized that Jerry Schilling had somehow disappeared. They searched and found him under a pile of clothes in Elvis's closet. Then they became fascinated by a large aquarium containing two or three fish, which appeared to them as an ocean teeming with fish. After a while Priscilla broke into tears. She dropped to her knees in front of Elvis and said, "You really don't love me. You just say you do." She then accused Larry and Jerry of not liking her, and called herself ugly. Eventually, that mood passed. The movie *The Time Machine* came on television. Elvis became fascinated by it. He asked for a pizza and spent most of the trip eating, while watching the film and observing his fellow trippers.
>
> At dawn they went outside. The rising sun created rainbows in the moist air that left them dazzled, and they examined dewdrops on the leaves. Then they got down on the lawn to inspect individual blades of grass. They could see the veins, and they watched the grass breathing slowly, in and out. They told each other how lucky they

were to be such friends. The experience fascinated Elvis and Priscilla, but they found LSD much too powerful and neither tried it again. Elvis's ability to sample and disregard marijuana and LSD no doubt reinforced his own feeling of mastery over such temptations. As a rule he detested drug use. He often expressed amazement that Hank Williams had died of an overdose. He found it incomprehensible that someone so intelligent and successful could fall prey to drugs. Yet the sad irony is that even in the mid-sixties he was starting a slide toward the same fate. He was blind to the process because his drugs came in the form of legal medications prescribed for him by doctors. [21]

Elvis was desperate to understand his unique gifts and calling in life, and devoured books that went beyond the Bible in hopes of providing an answer. Sadly, in the end, no belief system could divert Elvis from his own path toward self-destruction. Despite his spiritual quest, the perishing of the physical frame was one thing Elvis knew couldn't be conquered. Even if he successfully faked his own death, the reaper would still eventually show up one day to collect. But what if his daughter had known all along her father was alive? And what if the greatest artist of the next generation sought to learn the secrets from her? So that when it came his time to "die" he could successfully fake his own death, too!

8.
The Michael Jackson Connection

Everywhere I turn, no matter where I look,
The system's in control, it's all ran by the book,
I've got to get away so I can clear my mind,
Xscape is what I need, away from electric eyes
— Michael Jackson

A man's gift makes room for him,
and brings him before great men.
— Proverbs 18:16

The colored folks been singing it and playing it just like I'm doin' now, man, for more years than I know. I got it from them.
— Elvis

Lisa Marie Presley is the most famous only child in the world. The daughter of Elvis and the sole heir to his money-making empire, she's never had to work a day in her life. She's even cashed in on her father's name and recorded a few albums, some of which astonishingly managed to go platinum. She's produced films, done a little acting and even married the 'King of Pop,' Michael Jackson. A proud mother and eternal torchbearer of the Presley name, Lisa Marie has remained famous and intriguing simply for being the daughter of Elvis. But is she the "real" Lisa Marie or an imposter? Swedish scientist Hakan Borglund and investigative reporter Annika Sundbaum-Melin have been searching for the truth on this matter since 1990. They are convinced that Lisa Marie is a fraud and Elvis' real daughter disappeared in 1978. Borglund is of the opinion that the Lisa Marie Presley portrayed in the press is a

Lisa Marie at her father's funeral (Anouk1998 Fanpop.com)

Lisa Marie nine years-old (ElvisPresleymusic.com.au)

double, and has done a facial analysis comparing pictures of a nine-year-old Lisa Marie with modern ones. He was shocked to find that Lisa Marie's skull appeared to shrink more than 13 percent after puberty. It's scientifically impossible for a skull to shrink during the aging process. Greger Johnson, a biologist at the

Lisa with Elvis at party (ElvisPresleynews.com)

Lisa with Elvis in car 1977 (Elvis-collectors.com)

University of Lund, agrees with Borglund's theory that the person now calling herself Lisa Marie isn't the same little girl as the one shown in the pictures.

Maybe the need for a double was a calculated move by the family. It's postulated that the real Lisa Marie was kept hidden from the public eye due to serious kidnapping threats when Lisa Marie was a little girl. She made her last public appearance at Elvis' funeral service as a nine year old. Upon turning 18 in 1986, Lisa Marie flashed by in a few American magazine appearances then disappeared again. In 1988 she married Danny Keough, whom she met at the Church of Scientology. A year later she appeared in the press after giving birth to a daughter, and then again in 1992 after having another child. In 1993, *People Weekly* reported that Lisa Marie was living with her family in a three-bedroom apartment in Hollywood without bodyguards. When she turned 25 she was eligible for her inheritance, then worth close to a hundred million dollars. She turned the inheritance down, claiming not to be mature enough to handle it. Waiting for another five years,

18 year-old Lisa Marie with her mother in 1986
(ElvisPresleymusic.com.au)

she postponed the massive allowance while her mother and the Church of Scientology ran the Graceland empire from behind the scenes. Lisa Marie's turning to Scientology had a lot to do with the influence of John Travolta. Lisa Marie loved the actor, and Elvis even arranged for her to meet him when she was a little girl. With both her mother and favorite movie star acting as Scientology role models, it wouldn't take long for her to also come under the cult's spell, a move that would have no doubt infuriated Elvis, who once said after attending a Scientology meeting, "Fuck those people. All they want is my money."

In 1994 Dee Presley, the woman Vernon Presley fell in love with in Germany and married in 1960, admitted live on TV during the Elvis *Tribute from Memphis* that Priscilla hadn't allowed her to meet Lisa Marie since 1978. There's also the strange case of Lisa Johansen, a Swedish woman who sued the Presley estate for 130 million dollars, claiming that she was "the real Lisa Marie

Presley" who was forcibly exiled to Sweden after the death of her father and replaced by an imposter. But Johansen's memoir, *I, Lisa Marie*, was trashed after she refused to take an agreed-upon DNA test for her publisher, despite already accepting a $200,000 advance. Lisa Marie (or her double) had stayed very quiet and pretty mysterious, away from the public eye, until shocking the world by controversially marrying Michael Jackson in 1994. The marriage in the tropical Dominican Republic was universally seen as a cheap publicity stunt. A half-naked Lisa Marie appeared in the Michael Jackson video for the song "You are Not Alone," an awkward video but overall good song and maybe the only artistic highlight of their brief courtship. The marriage was a joke and has since proven to be nothing more than a hoax. The "wedding" took place in a Justice of the Peace's living room in the remote town of La Vega. Lisa Marie gave a fake passport number and spelled her first or last name wrong in four different ways while writing in the register that she was an actress, despite never having appeared once in a film, or even acting on any stage anywhere, at any time.

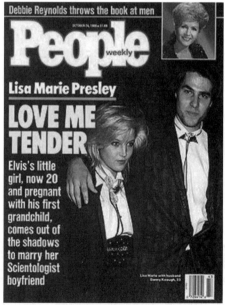

Lisa Marie comes out of the shadows and into Scientology 1988
(*People*)

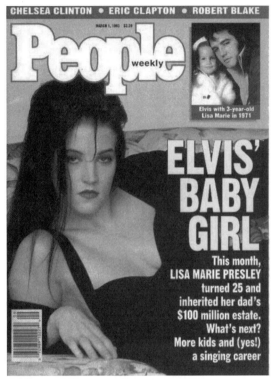

Lisa Marie turns 25 (*People*)

Of course in the days before the internet a well-rehearsed fake wedding was much easier to pull off. Former island resident and English editor for a Dominican newspaper, Tom Paine, writes (reprinted from his article without correction):

> According to the official wedding registration book and the JP's newspaper interview in his living room, the "wedding" took place at 10:00am in that same place, the living room in the JP's home. But hotel records show that Presley and Jackson, along with Presley's Scientology entourage were staying, in separate rooms, in separate buildings, at Casa de Campo, a resort more than 4 and 1/2 hours drive away, over unpaved and unmarked roads through the mountains. To get to the JP's home in La Vega at 10am, they would have had to have left their hotel no later than 5:30am. In 1994, many years before the toll

road through the mountains was built, the only way to get from Casa de Campo to La Vega (and back) was to drive west from the resort and pass through the incredible morning rush hour traffic jam that is Santo Domingo.

Because there were few actually working traffic lights in that city in those days, every intersection in that city of two and one-half million people was a battle ground. Once you fought your way through that and out the western side of the city, you must turn north and cross two mountain ranges (close to one mile high) on poorly paved – and sometime never paved – roads that lack road signs or directions. Until a toll road was built in the early part of the 21st Century, there was no other road. There are no restaurants along the way. No public toilets. No gasoline stations. It is a rugged, even dangerous trip in day light; at night Dominicans are wise to avoid it – and do. The 4 and 1/2 hours assigned to their alleged trip assumes no stops for food or rest. It assumes never getting lost. It assumes never needing to ask directions in Spanish. It may be hard to believe here in 2013, but in those days, the early 1990s – and for many years to come – there were no cell phones in that country. So how these strangers navigated right to his door remains one of the epic mysteries of modern times. According to the Justice of the Peace who claims he married them in his living room – but has no photos of them ever being in his home – there were only four adults (Michael, Lisa and the two witnesses) and a "very young baby." He says they arrived in a white van, at his home at 10:00am. He specifically states that they were alone, without a driver or interpreter.

No one, including the JP, has ever tried to explain how they knew him or why they chose him, so far away and unknown outside his home town, instead of all the many alternatives they passed on their alleged journey. Why did they not use one of the JPs who regularly

ELVIS BLASTS SCIENTOLOGY: 'That s.o.b. group —all they want is my money'

Lisa Marie was the apple of Elvis's eye before he died 20 years ago and his old friends say he would be horrified at his little girl's involvement with the sect.

Continued from Page 5

cause she desperately wanted to live close to the church. It was in that house that she collapsed in pain and was eventually taken to nearby Morton Plant Hospital, not long after undergoing the Scientology "cleansing" ritual.

During her hospital stay, STAR has learned that the 100-lb. young woman had an alarmingly high cholesterol level of 490. Doctors say healthy cholesterol levels usually average around 200.

The Scientology cleansing program can consist of ingesting megadoses of vitamins and sitting for hours in saunas, which can cause dehydration.

According to Dr. Victor Herbert, a professor at New York's Mount Sinai hospital, starvation and malnutrition can dramatically increase cholesterol levels.

"If these conditions continue, it can be life-threatening," says Herbert. "It can cause blood clotting, heart attacks and strokes. She is killing herself."

Doctors also discovered that Lisa Marie is suffering from Epstein Barr syndrome, also known as Chronic Fatigue syndrome, an energy-sapping ailment that doctors have found difficult to explain. Cher, Nicollette Sheridan and Peggy Lipton are just some of the stars who have been plagued by the

Lisa Marie paid $1.5 million for this house in Clearwater, Fla., so she could live near the Church of Scientology.

Police took her to Morton Plant Hospital for psychiatric evaluation, but within an hour a group of Scientologists turned up at her bedside. Despite a doctor's protests, they persuaded her to sign herself out, saying they would take care of her at their headquarters, the Fort Harrison Hotel.

Seventeen days later, on Dec. 5, 1995, a Scientologist was delivered McPher-

He says Lisa McPherson was trying to get out when she died, and claims in the lawsuit her death was caused by a church technique called "introspection rundown."

"In such cases the Scientologists followed a program of keeping the person in isolation till they snap out of it. But Lisa would not listen to them, and her health went down and down and down until she slipped into a coma."

Old friends of Elvis are concerned about Lisa Marie's dramatic involve-

jeans and flannel shirt, but all she would have on was one of the skimpy hospital gowns.

"Nurses and other staff would walk in and he'd have his arm around her or cradling her head, and they'd be whispering with their faces close together.

"He was on top of the cover usually, and she'd be half hanging out from under the cover with just the gown on.

"They slept together nearly every night. He'd be there in bed with her at

Elvis blasts Scientology (*The Star*)

officiate at Casa de Campo weddings? Why not one from the nearby town of Romana, or even Santo Domingo? The alleged witnesses on the "wedding license" were Lisa's Scientology "minder" who calls herself Darlene Love and her husband who happens to be the brother of Lisa Marie's "former" husband. They were allegedly accompanied, during that 9-hour round-trip trip by a baby "less than a year old." That detail was provided by the JP during his interview. Yet, no baby is listed in any records of immigration, the hotel or the airport...

There was only one car rental company at Casa de Campo that offers white vans. One was rented by Darlene Love at that agency at their desk in the lobby of the Casa de Campo hotel, using her personal American Express credit card. It was the only white van rented out by any of the four agencies at Casa de Campo during that time. For a small fee, the clerk provided a reporter with a photo

Michael and Lisa Marie at EuroDisney 1994 (AFP/Disney)

copy of that rental agreement and the Amex receipt. After the rental agency confirmed that this was the same van, it was photographed extensively to confirm its identity and its minimalist features. No air conditioning, no seat belts, un-padded seats.

This is the vehicle in which four adults and one infant allegedly spent a total of 9 hours, going and coming from Casa de Campo to La Vega and back during one day. The rental record says the van actually traveled fewer than 100 miles during that rental, less than 25% of the alleged round trip from the resort at Casa de Campo to the JP's home in La Vega… To arrive at the JP's home at 10am, the van would have had to leave the hotel no later than 5:30am and travel non-stop. It's pitch dark at that hour on that date. The roads have no lighting, are badly made, with huge potholes and absolutely no road signs of any kind. Virtually no one in the DR dares use those roads at that hour except to travel a few hundred yards in their own area. Long stretches of the roads through the high mountains towards La Vega are un-paved. Yet, here we have the claim that four foreigners, none of whom speak Spanish and who have never before been in that country, left their resort at 5:30 (in the dark) and drove through the mountains in that un-air-conditioned van – with a baby on board, too. No seat belts. No padding. We are speaking of some of the wealthiest people in the world and they did not spend a few bucks to hire an experienced local driver/interpreter? As you know, people like Jacko and Lisa never go anywhere without bodyguards, but they supposedly did that wild trip in a foreign country, without even a single bodyguard? No stopping for food or rest if you want to make the round trip in that time... Strange thing is, room service records back at the hotel show that breakfast was delivered and eaten by persons in each of the rooms rented to the various people in those rooms, at varying times between 8am and 11am, while they were allegedly on that arduous trip...

Oh, and did I mention they "returned" to the airport at Casa de Campo that very same day and took off in a Sony-operated jet a few minutes after 12 noon? To do that, means they made the four-and-a-half return trip from La Vega starting at 10:30 in slightly more than an hour and a half. Yet they also managed to pack up their rooms, check out of the hotel and get to the airport and clear through Immigration and climb aboard the jet. No lunch. No bathroom break. No phone calls. (No showers? Yeeww.) The Noon departure of that jet, and its passenger list detailing the presence of the same four adults (and no baby), plus the jet's crew, are recorded in the plane's log filed in the USA with the Federal Aviation Authority. The airport control tower supports that entry. But, there's even more evidence that knocks down any theory that the airplane's log might have been falsified or mistaken. It also proves who was actually on that airplane.

All air traffic in and out of the Dominican Republic is under the control of the Dominican Military. A ranking officer must personally record and approve every such event, complete with the plane's official ID and the passenger list. They are especially interested in the private planes that might be used to move drugs or illegal travelers. On that particular day, as the Sony-operated jet was taxiing to its starting point for takeoff, the Colonel on duty saw the name Michael Jackson on the manifest. In an interview for this story, he stated that he already had known Jacko was in the country because the previous day, the country's leading daily newspaper (Listin Diario) had published a front page story, complete with a standard publicity photo of Michael, repeating the rumor that Jackson was at Casa de Campo to discuss performing in the Amphitheater at Altos de Chavon (part of the 17,000-acre Casa de Campo property). That day-old newspaper was lying on the Colonel's desk as he read the Sony-jet passenger manifest and saw the name Michael Jackson. He picked his phone and called the airport tower, telling them to hold the plane at its starting position and ordering the pilot to shut down the engine, open the door and lower the stairs.

He has that authority to demand and hold, for inspection, any civilian aircraft. Those officers exercise that authority whenever they wish. He then jumped in his jeep and raced the few hundred yards to the plane. He had the newspaper with him. Today was his teen-daughter's birthday and he was going to bring her Jackson's autograph. That's exactly what he did. He showed this reporter that newspaper, with the Jackson photo on the front page and his distinct (and verified) autograph. He allowed it to be photographed. He also mentioned there were three other adults on the plane (whom the manifest confirms were Presley, Love and her husband – and no baby) but he had no interest in them and did not speak with them. He had no idea he was exposing the hoax. He then allowed the plane to leave. The log of the airport tower, and the Colonel's official report and the airplane's log all agree, that the plane with MJ on it took off shortly after 12 noon... Now, let's return to the so-called homemade video of the "wedding" that was shown on the Diane Sawyer show. More than any other evidence, is the most convincing evidence of a deliberate hoax and fraud. That home video scene was shot in a hotel room at Casa de Campo, not the JP's living room. This reporter went to that hotel and with the help of the manager ($50 bucks can get you a lot in that country) and found that exact room. Using a copy of that Diane Sawyer interview video, it was confirmed that we had the right room. Our cameraman recreated the home video showing every detail in the original. [22]

Michael and Lisa Marie in Budapest 1994 (AFP/Getty)

Whether the wedding was real or not, the real question is why did the 'King' of pop want to marry the 'King' of rock's daughter? Despite the carnival atmosphere of the whole affair, there appeared to be a genuine affection on the part of Jackson toward Lisa Marie. On June 26, 2009, Lisa Marie Presley blogged:

> Years ago Michael and I were having a deep conversation about life in general. I can't recall the exact subject matter but he may have been questioning me about the circumstances of my Father's Death. At some point he paused, he stared at me very intensely and he stated with an almost calm certainty, "I am afraid that I am going to end up like him, the way he did." I promptly tried to deter him from the idea, at which point he just shrugged his shoulders and nodded almost matter of fact as if to let me

know, he knew what he knew and that was kind of that. [23]

Which "idea" was she trying to deter him from? If she was referring to an early death led by a dependency on prescription drugs (which Jackson had) then maybe "thought" would have been a more suitable word. Instead she chose "idea," which changes the entire meaning of what she was expressing in her blog post. Could it be that Lisa Marie was trying to deter Jackson from the idea of faking his own death like her father supposedly had? After all, Michael Jackson was obsessed with Elvis Presley and was 100% convinced that the King had indeed successfully faked his own death. Was this the reason Jackson became close with Lisa Marie? What did he discover? Maybe Lisa Marie told him the truth?

Michael Jackson thumbs up at Grammy's (AFP/Getty)

On June 25, 2009 Michael Jackson died and nearly took the Internet with him. His death was so unbelievable that it crashed the web worldwide. Like Elvis, Jackson was a highly gifted artist and seeker of esoteric knowledge who also asked himself that eternally mysterious question, "why me?" He was also a good person who was kindhearted and giving, despite being alienated from the normal world and looked upon as a freak. Later when Jackson started revealing truths in his songs like "They Don't Care About Us," the Illuminati tried to ruin him.

The parallels between the two stars are freaky. Both were

born to extreme poverty, but became massive global music icons selling hundreds of millions of records each. Author and Elvis historian Alanna Nash says, "Like Elvis, Jackson unified black and white listeners, and made startlingly important, memorable, and era-defining music. Jackson was also a completely luminous performer—you couldn't take your eyes off of him—and part of it was because you sensed that this was an extraordinarily damaged boy-man, again, like Elvis, a Peter Pan, a *puer aeternus* [Latin for "eternal boy"]. Where Elvis co-created a musical art form, Michael largely built on one. Where Elvis changed sexual mores in the conservative wake of World War II, Michael only made shocking crotch-grabbing movements. And where Elvis, expanding on James Dean's work, harnessed a burgeoning youth culture, Michael only drew more attention to it. He did it brilliantly but his cultural impact pales in comparison to Presley's. There will always be throngs of people who will mourn and revere Jackson. But because his personal life was so outsized, peculiar, and tainted with scandal far more lurid than Presley's drug abuse, I can't see

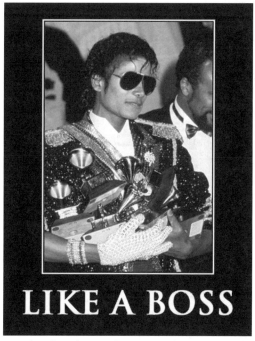

Michael Jackson Like a Boss (Tastemaker)

him morphing into the Disney zed figure that Elvis has become. It's far easier to overlook Elvis's peccadilloes than Michael's. Elvis was beautiful, sexy, and fun. Michael was sweet, strange, and sad. Who wants to see that on a lunchbox?" [24]

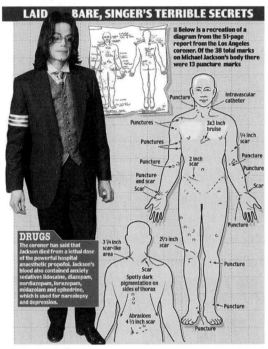

Michael Jackson Autopsy diagram *(Daily Mail)*

While Jackson blazed his own path to pop immortality, his death was so shockingly similar to Elvis' that it raises the question of whether it was faked. Some peculiar similarities are:

1. Both their deaths were claimed to be drug and heart related.
2. They both died at home.
3. They were both taken to the hospital by ambulance, even though already dead.
4. Both deaths led to an investigation into their doctors.
5. Both deaths were announced by family members—Elvis'

126

by Vernon Presley, Michael's by his older brother Jermaine.

6. In both cases the personal doctor was at the scene when the EMTs arrived.

7. The autopsy results in both cases are questionable.

8. Both were entombed in unmarked graves. Elvis' coffin was later reburied at Graceland; Michael's tomb remains unmarked to this day.

9. Their names were not mentioned in the 911 calls.

10. Both were buried in coffins that were flown in from other states.

11. Money, jewelry and various personal items went missing from both their homes after their deaths.

12. Both had foreign managers at the time of their death.

13. Both were highly interested in numerology and occult dates.

The similarities between Michael Jackson and Elvis Presley become weirder when examining their "deaths" as nothing more than elaborate hoaxes. From day one, multiple sources—media heads, family, and friends—had been listing the parallels between MJ's and Elvis' deaths. Details emerged on how Jackson spent much of his life emulating Elvis in multiple facets of his life, his art, his music, his clothes, his associations, and his spiritual beliefs. Did he even emulate Elvis' death? Jackson spent such an overwhelming amount of time emulating Elvis' last six months of life during his own last six months that it becomes too much of a coincidence to overlook. Was Jackson intending to outdo Elvis? Both were master showmen and extremely capable of pulling off a giant hoax. Did Michael Jackson follow in the footsteps of the King and fake his own death, too? Or was he murdered by the Illuminati instead of the mob?

Coroners' reports suggested that Michael Jackson was mostly bald other than a patch of peach fuzz on his head, and that the right side of his face and the bridge of his nose were caved in. However, when looking at the image of MJ being carried to the ambulance,

Michael Jackon's closet (*TMZ*)

you can see his face is undamaged and nose still in place. Meaning he didn't receive mouth-to-mouth resuscitation as reported, which requires one to pinch the nose while providing a stream of steady breaths into the mouth. Supposedly this resuscitation fractured his ribs, yet his wig remained in place on his head, and he even appeared to be wearing non-running eye makeup. For a dead man on his way to the hospital, Michael Jackson looked pretty damn good, much like the slim Elvis had while lying in that 900- pound coffin. This famous last photo has since proven to be photoshopped by longtime Jackson family lawyer and confidant, Brian Oxman, based on evidence gathered from the Michael Jackson Hoax Forum.

While Elvis' room was suspiciously devoid of any excess pill bottles, with carpets scrubbed and cleaned to perfection, Jackson's

Michael Jackon's bedroom (LAPD)

Elvis in the 1967 movie *Charro*. (MGM)

Elvis with Larry Geller in Hawaii 1977
(Larry Geller)

at Elvis in car with girl
(AFP/Getty)

Elvis in DEA jogging suit (The Presley Assignment)

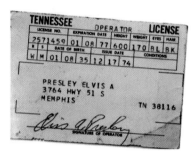

Elvis' expired driver's license
(Lindahoodsigmontruth.com)

Elvis photographed two months after his "death" -
Lindahoodsigmontruth.com

Elvis & Jesse – The Slanted Collar Bone

Note the sharp slant of the collar
bone in Elvis images, including X-ray
taken on Sept. 12, 1973 and this
photo of Jesse's collarbone. (Note
upper torso build/shape in general).

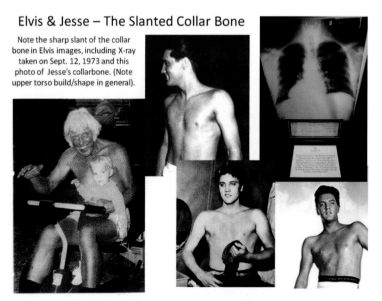

Elvis as Jesse? - Lindahoodsigmontruth.com

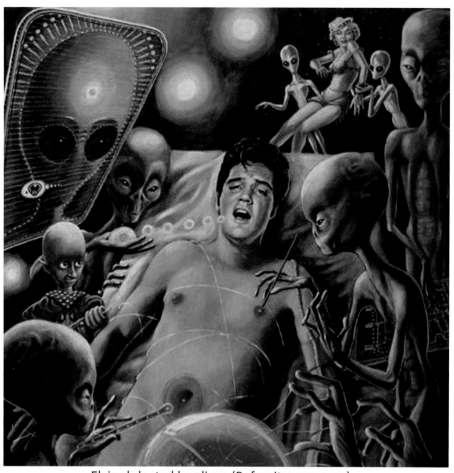
Elvis abducted by aliens (Beforeitsnews.com)

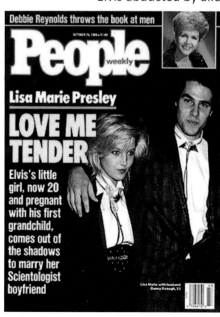

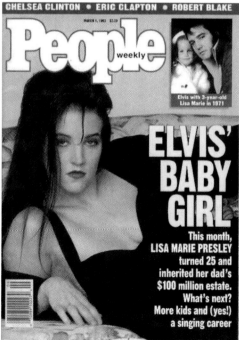

id Lisa Marie really marry Michael Jackson?

Michael's kids related to Elvis? (SimPattyk)

Paris
JACKSON, 14
THE KING OF
POP'S DAUGHTER

"My grandmother [Katherine Jackson] doesn't like it when I wear makeup. I can understand why—foundations aren't always good for your skin. When I spend the weekend at my friend's house, we usually have one night where we wash our faces and use those nose things for our pores. They're really cool!"
BEAUTY ICONS "Halle Berry and Beyoncé. Beyoncé is like an angel. She's one of the most beautiful women I've ever seen."

124 May 7, 2012 PEOPLE

Is Paris Jackson related to Elvis? *(People)*

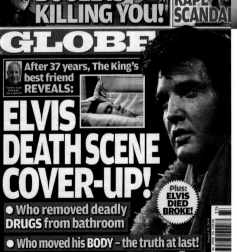

KATE WARNS DRUNKEN HARRY:
BOOZE IS KILLING YOU!

Keith Urban caught up in RAPE SCANDAL

GLOBE

After 37 years, The King's best friend REVEALS:

ELVIS DEATH SCENE COVER-UP!

Plus: ELVIS DIED BROKE!

● Who removed deadly **DRUGS** from bathroom

● Who moved his **BODY** – the truth at last!

Elvis continues to make the news as in this August, 2014 issue of *Globe*.

Michael Jackon's baby shrine (LAPD)

was the opposite with pill bottles on the floor, and no apparent attempts at cleaning. Jackson's room was a mess, littered with oxygen tanks, medical gloves, an IV stand with a saline drip bag, water bottles, a bizarre shrine of baby pictures, a statue of naked children, a butcher knife, and sticky notes and papers inscribed with everything from inspirational quotes, lyrics, and overall general musings to the addresses of all the nearest pharmacies. Michael even slept with a baby's doll and kept an assortment of masks and children's costumes.

The Jackson family refused to do an open-casket memorial service for Michael, claiming that his face had suffered injuries from the resuscitation attempts, despite the last known photo showing him to be looking intact. They obviously rejected the open viewing because there was no body, and they chose to avoid a wax-in-the-casket spectacle (much harder to pull off in 2009) a la the Elvis burial. Most of Michael Jackson's personal staff were fired weeks before his "death," and some immediately after, much like the firing of Elvis' entourage prior to his passing. Michael's death stunt looks more and more like a hoax when examining the video of him being transferred from UCLA to the coroner's office. You can clearly see the body on the stretcher actually rise up and move. Even his arrival at UCLA was suspicious, as you can see him being covered up and shielded by a staff of people after he exits the ambulance and before he enters the hospital. Michael Jackson's death certificate was not signed by a physician. Conrad

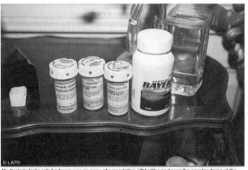

Medicated: Jackson's bedroom was an array of prescription pill bottles and over-the-counter drugs at the time of his death in June 2009

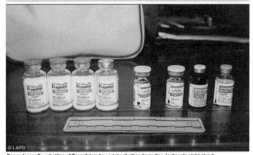

Dependency: Four bottles of Propofol and a variety of other drugs line Jackson's night stand

Michael Jackon's drugs (LAPD)

Murray refused to sign it, as did the physicians at the coroner's office. It's presumed that the examined dead body was actually one of Michael's sickly frail doubles.

Janet Jackson and other family members removed some of Michael's belongings from the rented Los Angeles mansion that he died in one day prior to the LAPD showing up to launch an investigation. But for some strange reason the family decided not to take the pill bottles, IV stands, or oxygen tanks? They even left his iconic jackets hanging in the closet. Keep in mind, when Elvis died, his house had been suspiciously cleansed and all the drugs were gone before the police arrived. So if Michael's belongings had already been removed, what exactly did the LAPD find? And how do we know that these things weren't planted there after the fact?

Conrad Murray had been reminded in an email from insurance titan AEG who paid his exorbitant $150,000 a month salary (AEG, not MJ) only 11 (a significant occult number) days before Michael died. A couple months prior to his death, Michael passed a five-hour insurance-related fitness test with flying colors. So why the sudden need for a cardiologist? Conrad Murray was a shady Las Vegas physician and rumored Freemason, a perfect candidate to be the scapegoat in Michael Jackson's death, especially if the Illuminati heads behind AEG wanted Michael Jackson dead. After all, as of June 25, 2014, Jackson has proven to be worth more dead than alive—posthumously raking in over a billion dollars since 2009. Taking advantage of his drug habit, it would have been easy for AEG to arrange for the hired doctor to administer a lethal dose of Propofol. The doctor would be set up to take the fall, but would get off relatively light for committing murder. Dr. Murray flashed an enormous number of Masonic hand symbols during the trial, and was let out of prison after only a year and a half. His handlers at AEG were sued unsuccessfully by Michael Jackson's mother Katherine, who held them responsible for her son's death. Any hopes Katherine had were quickly crushed when Dr. Murray refused to testify against his former bosses. He knew better.

Like Elvis, Jackson was an expert pill popper and drug adept, and reliant on prescription drugs for much of his adult life. Jackson even wrote a song called "Morphine" and definitely didn't need any medical advice from Conrad Murray, a man who claimed to be his "father figure" after a relatively short time. When revising Jackson's insurance policy for the 2009 London concerts, AEG bet heavily on an accidental death for Michael—not a natural one. Within accidental death bylaws, death ensuing from overdose and drug abuse is covered. So when this insurance policy was being drafted, did AEG have a premonition that Michael would die within a few months from a prescription drug overdose? Maybe Michael was aware of this plot and began to prepare his real final act—not a series of 50 concerts that he might not even be able to pull off, but the great death hoax instead. Before the scheduled July opening of the 50-show "This Is It" tour at the O2 arena in London, Michael repeatedly said, "See you in July." And just five days before July 1st he actually died, guaranteeing continual news coverage of his life, along with his music being played everywhere across the globe, throughout the month of July!

But his "death" gets stranger, and so does the man. Michael was obsessed with mannequins, and had them placed all around his homes. He even contacted the famous anatomist Gunther von Hagens to have his body posthumously turned into a mannequin via von Hagens' "plastination" technique. But did he also have replicas of his body created while still alive? He was known to send mannequins on ambulance rides and on other weird voyages in order to fool with the paparazzi. Michael Jackson, like the rest of the elite, was obsessed with living forever. He thought of himself as Peter Pan, and even lived in a real-life Neverland. Legend says that he even slept in a hyperbaric chamber to remain youthful. He was a vegetarian and only ate one meal a day, for fear of being poisoned. Jackson had even told Lisa Marie exactly how he was going to die years before it happened. With his eccentric nature, he wanted to know how the world would react to finding out that he was dead, and wanted to witness this event firsthand. Like Elvis, Jackson also wanted to live a life where he could enjoy the common aspects of an ordinary "Joe Schmoe" existence, such as walking outside and going shopping, without attracting the circus. He was a master of disguises and might even have shown up at his own memorial service in one.

Michael Jackson had plenty of reasons to stage his own death, and used the London "comeback" gigs to drum up public interest for his epic finale, fully knowing he wouldn't need to perform at O2 because his "death" a few days before opening night would stop the concert series in its tracks. This in turn would send music and paraphernalia sales soaring, clearing his debts and providing him with a comfortable secret life on an island of his own choosing. While he lives incognito, leaked details relating to Jackson's death are purposely used to keep the public focused on the dead Michael, and on all the drugs he took, what the autopsy results were, on and on and on, all spun by the media to keep the official story going.

The real Michael Jackson never showed up at rehearsals

the night before his "death" at Staples Center; the dark footage showing him chewing gum has been proven to be of one of his doubles. If he wasn't practicing at the Staples Center, is this when Michael Jackson escaped to a private plane and left the public eye forever? An unmarked Lear Jet was seen leaving LAX on the eve of his death in Los Angeles. Meanwhile, back at the rented Jackson mansion, the much-rehearsed show was about to begin. The ball began rolling with the 911 call wherein the caller never said, "This is Michael Jackson's residence and Mr. Jackson needs immediate help," but instead spoke of a "gentleman" who was "not breathing." This set the stage for the act of taking the double, a mannequin or even a disguised MJ to the hospital in an ambulance. However, there was something strange about the ambulance. All LAFD ambulance vehicles are registered with more than just two numbers, proving this number 71 ambulance privately belonged to Michael Jackson. The popular celebrity news program *TMZ* reported that Jackson had died even before UCLA announced his death. How was that possible?

The subject of Michael Jackson's children is another bizarre piece of the death hoax puzzle. Jackson was adamant on maintaining privacy for them and always kept them covered up when out in public; however, just a few months before his "death" his children were fully unveiled to the world. His eldest daughter, Paris, has proven to be quite the actress, a career she has admitted to always wanting. Early footage shows her practicing crying on cue, and she made her big debut at it during Jackson's memorial service. But life in the spotlight quickly jaded the teenage girl, and Paris has since proved to be rather problematical, just like her father. In 2013 she made a stunning announcement warning the world about the dangers of the Illuminati before an alleged "suicide" attempt. Paris, now sixteen, is attending the $10 million Diamond Ranch Academy boarding school in Utah after spending a year in a California "rehab" facility. Her brothers, Prince Michael and Blanket, live with their guardian grandmother Katherine Jackson, and haven't had much speaking time with the media. They've been too busy practicing karate. Practicing karate? Yes, like

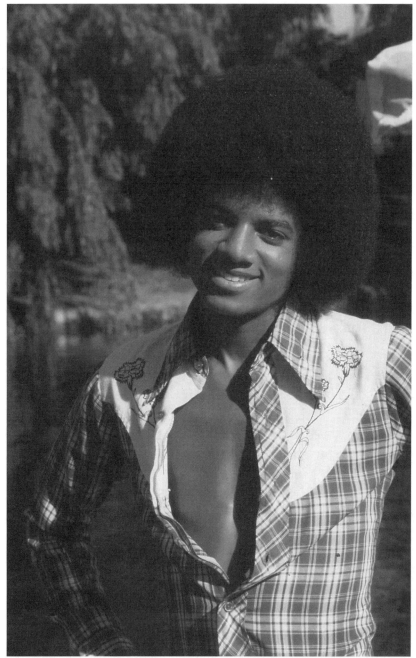

Michael in the 70's (Jacksons)(ElvisPresleymusic.com.au)

their grandfather Elvis used to do. Could the whole reason for Jackson's marriage to Lisa Marie have been to get her to agree to lend him some eggs, which Jackson could artificially inseminate thus creating a potential super artist child with both his and Elvis' DNA? He could have used Debbie Rowe as the surrogate mother to distract the media. When looking at Jackson's three children it's pretty easy to see the Elvis resemblance. What's missing is Jackson's resemblance. Let's be honest here, those kids are pretty damn white and Michael Jackson was not.

The lyrics of Jackson's song "Xscape" clearly state what Michael Jackson's intentions were, intentions that he put into practice with help from Lisa Marie. During their "marriage" she learned of Jackson's desire to escape like her father did, and it's possible she coached him on how to successfully stage such an event. Jackson got the goods from her on how Elvis' death was staged and successfully "sold" to the public by the media back in 1977, and now it was his turn to do the deed. Did Jackson successfully fake his own death in 2009 like Elvis might have in 1977?

Michael with bird (Jacksons)

135

Michael on Sesame Street (SesameWiki)

If so, the IRS wasn't going to get shafted when it came to the massive amounts of money the Jackson estate began accumulating after his "death." *The Guardian* reports:

> US government officials have opened a case against the estate of Michael Jackson, claiming that the singer's executors owe almost three quarters of a billion dollars in back taxes and penalties. According to documents obtained by the *Los Angeles Times*, there is a huge gap between executors' valuation of the Jackson estate and what has been calculated by government auditors. The estate claimed that when Jackson died in June 2009, his net worth was a mere $7m (£4.3m). The IRS (Internal Revenue Service) came to a figure about 160 times higher: $1.125bn (£76m). The difference is so big that the IRS has allegedly given the submission a gross valuation misstatement penalty, entitling it to an extra 20% in fines. Although it is well documented that Jackson was in debt at the time of his death, the singer still had huge financial resources: rights to his own back catalogue, rights to his likeness and name, plus the publishing catalogue for artists

including the Beatles, Hank Williams and Eminem. The Jackson estate is accused of undervaluing these holdings. Whereas the IRS pegged the value of the singer's likeness at $434.3m (£264.7m), executors claimed that it was worth just over $2,000 (£1,200). Jackson's stake in Sony/ATV Music Publishing—worth an estimated $469m (£285m), according to officials—was reportedly valued at "zero" dollars. The Jackson estate is also accused of skimping on its valuations of stocks, Rolls-Royces and master tapes. [25]

They've also been trying to recover Jackson's secret art collection valued close to a billion dollars. A crushing $700 million fine by the IRS will keep the financial power structure within Jackson's estate entangled for decades. Just think about it—since his "death" Jackson has generated close to $700 million and that's exactly how much the IRS wants! Even if you successfully fake your own death, you still can't avoid the dangling chainsaws of the Tax Man.

Time will reveal how Jackson's legend is looked upon in the future; reaction so far is nowhere near the hysterics reached in the wake of Elvis' vanishing. After his death, the 'Elvis lives!' hype continued to grow throughout the ensuing decades, with reports of him appearing all over the world. He even had time to act as an extra in the popular movies *Finding Graceland* and *Home Alone*! *Finding Graceland* was produced by Lisa Marie, who made a Freudian slip on Larry King's show saying "Elvis loves Football," implying that he was still alive. It's hard to say

Michael's kids related to Elvis? (SimPattyk)

137

Michael's kids like karate like Elvis? (SimPattyk)

whether Elvis faked his death or not. Simply put, Elvis disappeared from public view in late 1977 and was replaced by an onslaught of marketing merchandise and well-timed posthumous album releases, singing to the tune of hundreds of millions.

The Elvis-is-alive theory seems to be a case of what you want to believe. For the most part, the general public believes that Elvis left the building in the late 70s, but a small minority, fueled by a culture of conspiracy, stand firm that the King of Rock 'n' Roll is enjoying a triple cheeseburger dripping with bacon and peanut butter somewhere out in the wild blue yonder. On his last concert tour, an overweight Elvis famously warned his fans that his days of touring were numbered, saying, "I may not look good tonight, but I'll look good in my coffin." On a different occasion, also on the final tour, he said, "I know I look fat now and I'll look terrible for my TV special coming up. But I'll tell you this: I'll look good in my casket."

Yes, Elvis, your wax double sure did look good in that casket.

Paris Jackson (*People*)

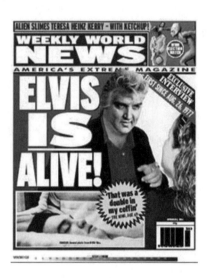

9.
Long Live the King

He walks in my mind like a shadow
Someone speaks his name and he appears
I can see his face in total darkness
Oh, he's everywhere
He left a memory that lives with me
A memory of how it used to be
And I remember all the things we used to share
Oh, he's everywhere
— Dolly Parton

Beloved, do not be surprised at the fiery trial when it comes upon you to test you, as though something strange were happening to you."
— Peter 4:12

I believe in the Bible. I believe that all good things come from God. I don't believe I'd sing the way I do if God hadn't wanted me to.
— Elvis

Long live the King? As baby boomers enter their twilight nights and the number of generations with actual firsthand memories of the King dwindles, what are we to make of Elvis' legacy in the first new decades of the 21st century? It's no secret that interest in Elvis Presley in Sin City is on the wane. Despite there being nearly 200 Las Vegas-area Elvis impersonators, their bookings have fallen by over 30% since 2010. So, too, has the number of weddings performed by an Elvis chaplain. A Las Vegas marriage tradition over the years is now on the rocks due to younger couples not being interested in a gimmicky marriage. Carrie Gaudioso, wedding coordinator for the Mon Bel Ami chapel says, "The whole Elvisy Vegas red carpet thing is, in my opinion, going out the door. That whole era is getting older. Almost all of our older renewals want an Elvis wedding. Our younger brides do not want cheesy, flashy, Elvis Vegas. They want something nice in their budget." [26]

The decline of Elvis interest in Las Vegas is likely due to the aging of the fan base. According to new studies, more than 40% of Las Vegas tourists are 50 or under, and are likely too young to have strong memories (or any memories) of Presley when he was alive. Despite this, the Presley brand is stronger than ever and shows no signs of slowing down. It was even acquired by Authentic Brands Group, which purchased the intellectual property rights associated with Elvis from Core Media Group in 2014. Authentic Brands already controls the Marilyn Monroe and Juicy Couture brands, and now with the global rights to a vast library of Elvis-related content secured, they should continue to dominate the pop art marketing world while securing Elvis' popularity amongst new generations.

New and old fans alike gather every August in Memphis and pay tribute to the King with a candlelight vigil on the anniversary of his death. Police estimate that over 40,000 people show up each year for this rock 'n' roll pilgrimage. In 2012, the 35th anniversary of Elvis' death, more than 75,000 people gathered to pay their respects. Elvis Presley Enterprises estimates that 30% of both Graceland tourists and the ten million Elvis fans on Facebook are under the age of 35. Graceland was even voted as number one in the Best Iconic American Attractions survey by *USA Today*. Fox is producing a new Elvis film based Peter Guralnick's biography *The Last Train to Memphis: The Rise of Elvis Presley*, with Kevin McDonald directing and Mick Jagger listed as one of the producers. A new film on Elvis should help spread his appeal to the next generation. However, it's hard to imagine anyone doing a better job portraying Elvis than Jonathan Rhys Meyers did in the excellent television miniseries from 2005, *Elvis: The Early Years*.

Elvis Presley's music came along at the perfect time, as the convergence of portable radios, credit cards, and crossover television appeal ushered in a new era of teenage consumerism. Pulitzer Prize-winning journalist David Halberstram explains:

> Presley's timing was nearly perfect. ... Parents might disapprove of the beat and of their children listening to what they *knew* was black music. But their disapproval only added to Presley's popularity and made him more of a hero among the young. Local ministers might get up in their churches (almost always well covered by local newspapers) and attack demon rock as jungle music and threaten to lead a crusade to have this Presley boy arrested if he dared set foot in their community (generally, there was no problem, their towns were too small for him to play). It did not matter: Elvis Presley and rock music were happening. A new young generation of Americans was breaking away from the habits of its parents and defining itself by its music. There was nothing the parents could do: This new generation was armed with both money and the new inexpensive appliances with which to listen to it. This was the new, wealthier America. Among the principal beneficiaries of that prosperity were the teenagers. They had almost no memory of a Depression and the great war that followed it. There was no instinct on their part to save money. Technology favored the young...In the early fifties a series of technological breakthroughs brought small transistorized radios that sold for $25 to $50. Soon an Elvis Presley model record player was selling for $47.95. Teenagers were asked to put $1 down and pay only $1 a week. Credit buying had reached the young. By the late fifties, American companies sold 10 million portable record players a year. In this new subculture of rock and roll the important figures of authority were no longer mayors and selectmen or parents; they were disc jockeys, who reaffirmed the right to youthful independence and guided teenagers to their new rock

143

heroes. The young formed their own community. For the first time in American life they were becoming a separate, defined part of the culture: As they had money, they were a market, and as they were a market they were listened to and catered to. Elvis was the first beneficiary. In effect, he was entering millions of American homes on the sly; if the parents had had their way, he would most assuredly have been barred. [27]

Elvis emerged from the fifties to become the biggest selling solo artist of all time. His cultural impact on music and on society at large is unmatched. He was able to take music with deep African-American roots and add his own flair to it while presenting it to the masses of white America and beyond. John Lennon once famously said, "Before Elvis there was nothing." And boy was he correct, meaning rock 'n' roll never existed at that level of popularity and, more importantly, at that level of sales. Elvis also knew where his roots were, as he told reporters from *Time* magazine in 1956, "The colored folks been singing it and playing it just like I'm doing now, man, for more years than I know. I got it from them. Down in Tupelo, Mississippi, I used to hear old Arthur Crudup bang his box the way I do now, and I said if I ever got to the place where I could feel how old Arthur felt, I'd be a music man like nobody ever saw." Elvis did not invent rock and roll. But he was an innovator, nonetheless, transfusing the popular white music of the fifties with black gospel, blues and soul music. And that transfusion was an important component of the anti-segregation sentiment that was brewing at the time, and that led ultimately to the Civil Rights Movement and desegregation in the South.

Elvis won the Grammy Lifetime Achievement Award at 36, and has sold over one billion records. Even in the world of digitally streaming music, Elvis Presley is still the King. According to SoundExchange, a performance rights organization that collects royalties from more than 2,000 digital music services, Presley ranks as the most frequently streamed artist of the past decade. He's also number two on the list of highest earning dead celebrities, raking in over $55 million in 2013. The cultural and musical legacy of Elvis Presley continues to grow. The public's fascination with him, mostly fueled by a conspiracy culture, keeps him interesting, but the everlasting power of his music has the ability to reach new fans and new generations unlike that of any other artist. The conspiracy theories surrounding how Elvis died—whether he was murdered, took an unintentional drug overdose, or perpetrated a massive hoax—will continue to be debated for decades to come. But this book was never about dying, it's about living, and after assessing the facts, including those that seem mysterious and out of place, it's apparent that, even if only in spirit, Elvis is still alive. Long live the King.

FOOTNOTES

1. "Remembering Elvis also as King of UFO's," Jeff Peckman, *Examiner.com*, August 16, 2010 http://www.examiner.com/article/ remembering-elvis-also-as-king-of-ufos

2. "The Mystery of Jesse Garon," Larry Geller, *Larry Geller's Blog*, February 4, 2011 http://www.elvispresleybiography.net/elvis-presley-hairstylist-larry-geller-blog/?p=60

3. Steve Dunleavy, *Elvis: What Happened?* (New York, NY: Ballantine, 1977)

4. "Nightmares are Linked to Creativity in New View," Dan Goleman, *New York Times*, October 23, 1984 http://www.nytimes. com/1984/10/23/science/nightmares-are-linked-to-creativity-in-new-view.html

5. Johnny Cash, *The Autobiography* (New York, NY: HarperOne, 2003)

6. "Mae Axton and Heartbreak Hotel," *Oklahoma Historical Society,* January 28, 2012 *http://www.okhistory.org/about/transcript. php?episodedate=2012-01-28*

7. "The Rise and Fall of Popular Music," Donald Clarke, *Donaldclarkemusicbox.com* http://www.donaldclarkemusicbox.com/ rise-and-fall/detail.php?c=15

8. "Quotes on Elvis," John Lennon http://johnlennonquotes.net/ john-lennon-quotes-about-elvis-presley.htm

9. "Life: Book Excerpt," Keith Richards, *New York Times*, November 4, 2010 http://www.nytimes.com/2010/11/14/books/review/ excerpt-life.html?_r=0

10. "The USSR Spent 1 Billion on Mind-control Programs," Jenni Ryall, *News Australia*, December 30, 2013 http://www.news.com. au/technology/science/exposed-the-soviet-union-spent-1-billion-on-mindcontrol-program/story-fn5fsgyc-1226790700498

11. "Elvis Uncovered," Ray Connolly, *Daily Mail* August 16, 2014, updated June 20, 2002 http://www.dailymail.co.uk/tvshowbiz/ article-124163/Elvis-uncovered.html

12. "Elvis Presley: the real Story on His Drug Abuse," Lasrever, *Live Leaks*, March 27, 2008 http://m.liveleak.com/view?i=73d_1206664864

13. "The Last photograph of Elvis" Phil Arnold, *ElvisBlog. net*, August 12, 2011 http://www.elvisblog.net/2011/08/12/the-last-photograph-of-elvis-alive/

14. "Proof That Elvis is Not Jesse," Mickey Moran, *The Presley Assignment*, December 11, 2013 http://www.thepresleyassignment.com/apps/photos/photo?photoid=187509781

15. "The Elvis Presley Conspiracy" Andrew W. Mayoras, *Probate Lawyer Blog*, March 1, 2010 http://www.probatelawyerblog.com/2010/03/the-elvis-presley-conspiracy-part-ii-the-background.html

16. "Lucy and Elvis in Las Vegas!" Terri Sundquist, *Promega Connections*, October 20, 2009 http://www.promegaconnections.com/lucy-and-elvis-in-las-vegas-a-summary-of-the-20th-international-symposium-on-human-identification/

17. "Elvis Mysteries," Mickey Moran, *The Presley Assignment*, December 27, 2012 http://www.thepresleyassignment.com/apps/blog/show/21457651-elvis-mysteries

18. "Elvis was Murdered by the Mob!" *National Enquirer*, October 12, 2011 http://www.nationalenquirer.com/celebrity/elvis-presley-was-murdered-mob

19. "John Lennon's Bible," Robert Rosen, February 5, 2006 http://robertrosen.blogspot.com/2006/02/john-lennons-bible-and-occult.html

20. "Larry Geller Interview Part 1," *Elvisinfonet.com*, September, 2003 http://www.elvisinfonet.com/gellar.html

21. "Elvis the Seeker," Gary Tillery, *Reality Sandwich* https://realitysandwich.com/180680/elvis_seeker/

22. "Michael Jackson/Lisa Presley Wedding Hoax," Tom Paine, *Pissing in the Soup*, May 13, 2013 http://pissinginthesoup.com/2013/05/14/the-fraudulent-wedding-of-michael-jackson-and-lisa-marie-presley/

23. "Lisa Marie Remembers Ex-husband Michael Jackson," Jocelyn Vena, *MTV News*, June 26, 2009 http://www.mtv.com/news/1614840/lisa-marie-presley-remembers-ex-husband-michael-jackson/

24. "Elvis and Michael Parallel Lives," *Elvisinfonet.com*, 2010 http://www.elvisinfonet.com/Michael_Jackson_Elvis_Presley.html

25. "Michael Jackson's Estate Taxed in Battle with IRS," Sean Michaels, *The Guardian*, February 10, 2014 http://www.theguardian.com/music/2014/feb/10/michael-jackson-estate-tax-battle-irs

26. "Fading Glory: Demand for Elvis Impersonators Isn't What It Used to Be," Laura Carroll, *Las Vegas Review-Journal*, September 7, 2013 http://www.reviewjournal.com/business/fading-glory-demand-elvis-impersonators-isnt-what-it-used-be

27. "How Elvis Presley Ushered in the Era of Teen Consumer Culture," Maria Popova, *Brainpickings.org*, April 11, 2013 http://www.brainpickings.org/index.php/2013/04/11/elvis-presley-teens-consumer-culture/

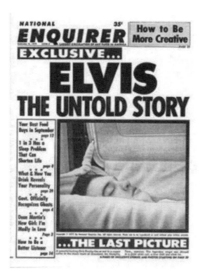

ELVIS PRESLEY: HIS STORY IN PICTURES
Written by Angus Allan, Illustrated by Arthur Ranson

153

Elvis signs a recording contract . . .

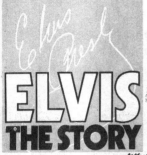

1954. THE END OF A WHOLE ERA OF POP MUSIC. 'SOFT' SINGERS LIKE DORIS DAY AND DEAN MARTIN WERE TOPPING THE CHARTS...

ROCK AND ROLL? PHONEY AND FALSE. PLAYED FOR THE MOST PART BY CRETINOUS GOONS!

...AND FRANK SINATRA WAS CHARACTERISTICALLY OUTSPOKEN ABOUT A RAW NEW MUSIC THAT SEEMED TO MANY TO BE AN ABSURD AND TEMPORARY CRAZE...

HOW WRONG HE WAS! IN TIME, SINATRA WAS DESTINED TO ENGAGE ELVIS FOR A SPECIAL SHOW AT AN ASTRONOMICAL $150,000 FOR A SIX MINUTE APPEARANCE!

THAT HOWEVER WAS IN THE FUTURE. AT HOME IN MEMPHIS, ELVIS TOOK A PHONE CALL FROM SAM PHILLIPS, BOSS OF SUN RECORDS...

YOU MADE A PRIVATE RECORD FOR YOUR MOM, THREE MONTHS AGO. SON, I LIKE IT. I WANT YOU TO RECORD SOMETHING ELSE...

I HUNG UP AND RAN FIFTEEN BLOCKS TO MR. PHILLIPS'S OFFICE BEFORE HE'D GOTTEN OFF THE LINE!

MUCH LATER, AT THE HEIGHT OF HIS FAME, ELVIS WAS FOND OF RECALLING HIS REACTION TO THAT CALL...

PHILLIPS HAD A GOOD TRACK RECORD FOR HUNCHES. HE'D GIVEN COUNTRY AND WESTERN SINGER JOHNNY CASH AND ROCKER JERRY LEE LEWIS WHO BECAME BIG STARS THEIR FIRST BREAKS...

I WANT YOU TO CUT "BLUE MOON OF KENTUCKY", AND "THAT'S ALL RIGHT, MAMA". THAT'S A BIG BOY CRUDUP NUMBER...

IT WAS WHEN A FLAMBOYANT EX-CARNIVAL PROMOTER NAMED 'COLONEL' TOM PARKER HEARD ELVIS'S MUSIC THAT THINGS BEGAN TO MOVE...

JUST LISTEN TO THIS. I'D SAY THIS BOY HAS A MILLIONS-WORTH OF TALENT!

ALWAYS PERSUASIVE, PARKER ENGINEERED A DEAL WITH THE GIANT RECORDING COMPANY, RCA-VICTOR. AND IN 1955, THEY BOUGHT ELVIS'S CONTRACT FROM SUN FOR $35,000...

YOU AND I, BOY, ARE GOING TO CONQUER THE WORLD!

YEAH, I KNOW IT.

THE DISCS WERE BIG LOCAL HITS BUT SUN RECORDS WERE HARDLY GEARED FOR NATIONWIDE DISTRIBUTION IN A COUNTRY AS HUGE AS THE USA! TWO MORE SINGLES FOLLOWED...

THINKING OF TAKING A PIECE OF THE ACTION, TOM?

3

157

Elvis's fame spreads to England . . .

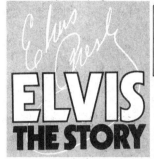

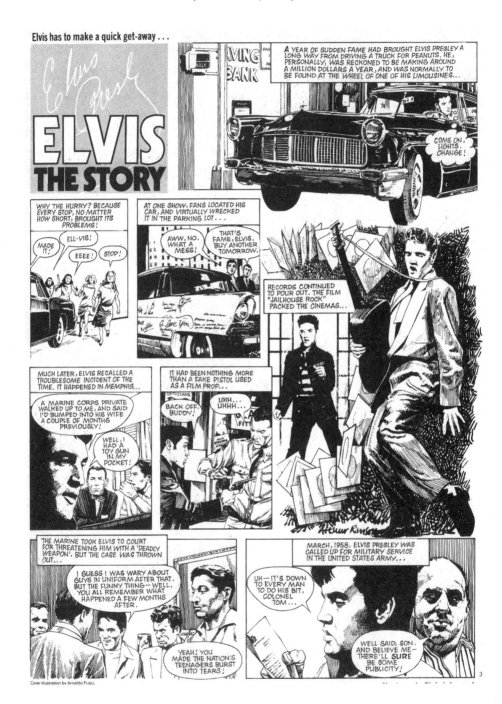

161

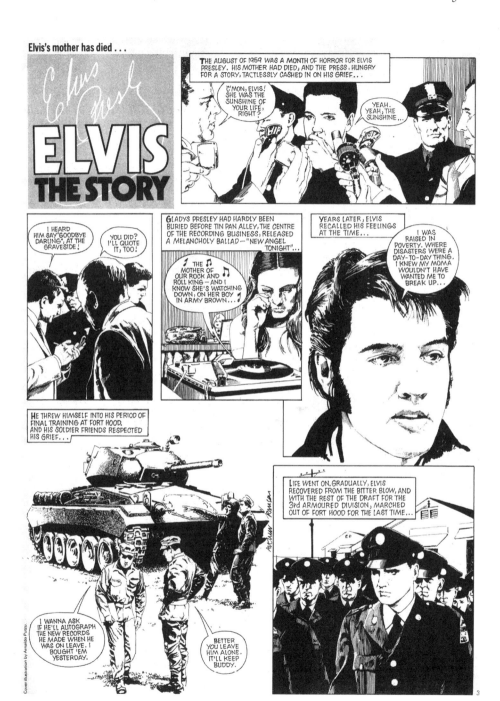

Elvis leaves the army — to even more Presley-mania!

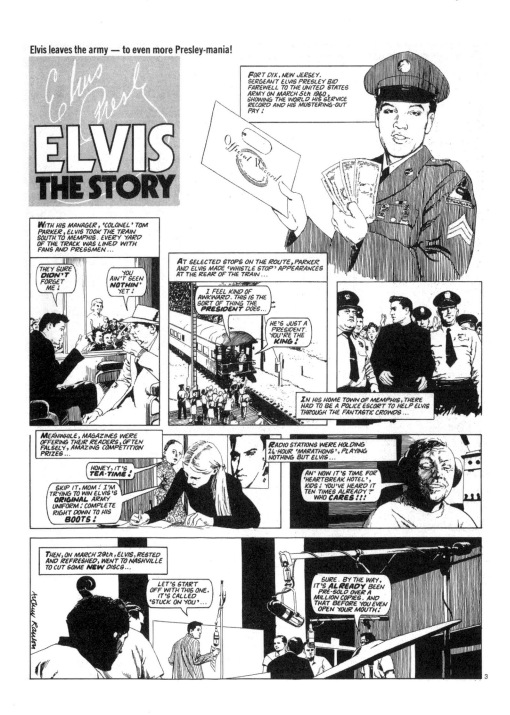

THERE HAD BEEN NO NEED FOR ELVIS TO WORRY ABOUT HIS POPULARITY AFTER HIS TWO YEARS IN THE ARMY. HIS STATUS WAS AS HIGH AS IT HAD ALWAYS BEEN, AND IT WAS A VERY CONFIDENT PRESLEY WHO WENT BACK INTO UNIFORM AGAIN—THIS TIME FOR PARAMOUNT'S CAMERAS AT HOLLYWOOD...

THE FILM WAS G.I. BLUES—WITH A FRANKLY HAMMY SORT OF PLOT AND A DEFINITE 'FAMILY' APPEAL. ELVIS WAS SHOT WITH BABIES...

HE SANG WITH PUPPETS...

...BUT I DON'T HAVE A WOODEN HEART...

HE EVEN TOOK IT ON THE CHIN TO MAKE FANS GASP WITH DISMAY...

G.I. BLUES SET THE SEAL ON ELVIS PRESLEY'S NEW IMAGE. THERE WERE MANY WHO REGRETTED THE DISAPPEARANCE OF THE OILY-HAIRED, HIP-TWITCHING, REBEL ROCKER...

I REALLY DUG THE WAY HE USED TO BE. HE'S STILL MY ELVIS, OF COURSE...

SURE! HE'S ALWAYS ELVIS! NOTHING CAN ALTER *THAT!*

WHILE THE FILM WAS BEING MADE, ROYALTY CAME TO SEE ELVIS ON SET. THE KING AND QUEEN OF THAILAND, NO LESS...

MORE IMPORTANTLY, THE PUBLIC WENT TO SEE THE FILM AT THE CINEMA. ONE OF THE MOVIE INDUSTRY'S ALL-TIME SMASH-HITS, IT GROSSED 4·3 MILLION DOLLARS IN THE U.S. AND CANADA ALONE...

IT WAS THEN THAT ELVIS DECIDED TO REALLY GO OUT ON A LIMB. HE DECIDED TO TEST HIMSELF AS A SERIOUS ACTOR—WIN OR LOSE!

175

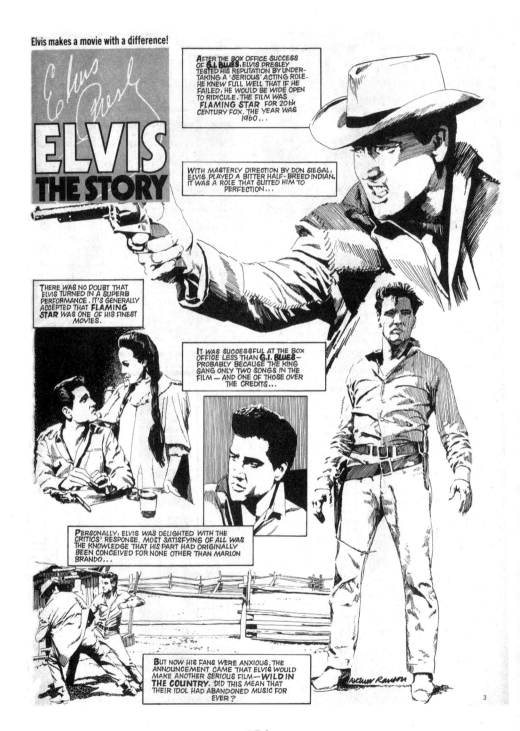

Elvis makes a movie with a difference!

ELVIS THE STORY

AFTER THE BOX OFFICE SUCCESS OF **G.I. BLUES**, ELVIS PRESLEY TESTED HIS REPUTATION BY UNDERTAKING A 'SERIOUS' ACTING ROLE. HE KNEW FULL WELL THAT IF HE FAILED, HE WOULD BE WIDE OPEN TO RIDICULE. THE FILM WAS **FLAMING STAR** FOR 20th CENTURY FOX. THE YEAR WAS 1960...

WITH MASTERLY DIRECTION BY DON SIEGAL, ELVIS PLAYED A BITTER HALF-BREED INDIAN. IT WAS A ROLE THAT SUITED HIM TO PERFECTION...

THERE WAS NO DOUBT THAT ELVIS TURNED IN A SUPERB PERFORMANCE. IT'S GENERALLY ACCEPTED THAT **FLAMING STAR** WAS ONE OF HIS FINEST MOVIES.

IT WAS SUCCESSFUL AT THE BOX OFFICE LESS THAN **G.I. BLUES** — PROBABLY BECAUSE THE KING SANG ONLY TWO SONGS IN THE FILM — AND ONE OF THOSE OVER THE CREDITS...

PERSONALLY, ELVIS WAS DELIGHTED WITH THE CRITICS' RESPONSE. MOST SATISFYING OF ALL WAS THE KNOWLEDGE THAT HIS PART HAD ORIGINALLY BEEN CONCEIVED FOR NONE OTHER THAN MARLON BRANDO...

BUT NOW HIS FANS WERE ANXIOUS. THE ANNOUNCEMENT CAME THAT ELVIS WOULD MAKE ANOTHER SERIOUS FILM—**WILD IN THE COUNTRY**. DID THIS MEAN THAT THEIR IDOL HAD ABANDONED MUSIC FOR EVER?

3

HIS PORTRAYAL OF A BITTER INDIAN HALF-BREED IN THE FILM 'FLAMING STAR' WON ELVIS RESPECT AS A STRAIGHT ACTOR. THE LOS ANGELES INDIAN TRIBAL COUNCIL MADE HIM A BLOOD-BROTHER IN REGARD FOR HIS 'CONSTRUCTIVE PORTRAYAL'...

NEXT CAME 'WILD IN THE COUNTRY', AND A MOODY, REBELLIOUS ROLE THAT SUITED ELVIS PERFECTLY.

IT HAS NEVER BEEN EXACTLY ESTABLISHED WHO CALLED A HALT TO THE KING'S CAREER AS A SERIOUS PLAYER. BUT BOX-OFFICE RECEIPTS WERE CERTAINLY THE REASON...

FACE IT. THESE FILMS HAVE MADE MONEY, YES. BUT THE MUSICALS MAKE MORE...

AND MORE IS BETTER, YES, SIR!

ELVIS FLEW TO HAWAII, FIRST TO MAKE A PUBLIC APPEARANCE AT PEARL HARBOR'S BLOCH ARENA...

HE SANG MOST OF HIS HITS, OLD AND NEW — AND THE FANS LOVED IT!

ELVIS, ELVIS!

WE LOVE YOU!

'UH-SINCE MAH BABY LEFT ME, AH FOUND A NEW PLACE TO DWELL —

DOWN THE END OF A LONELY ROAD — HEARTBREAK HOTEL...

IT'S NOW OR NEVER...

NONE OF THEM COULD HAVE GUESSED THAT THIS WAS THE LAST TIME ANYONE WOULD SEE ELVIS PERFORMING IN PERSON — FOR EIGHT LONG YEARS!

THAT NIGHT IN HAWAII MARKED THE BEGINNING OF A CURIOUS PERIOD WHERE BOTH SUCCESS AND DECLINE WENT, BAFFLINGLY, HAND-IN-HAND...

179

ONCE, BACK IN 1969, A KID FROM A CLAPBOARD SHACK IN TUPELO, MISSISSIPPI, HAD A DREAM. HE'D BEEN PHOTOGRAPHED IN A COWBOY OUTFIT...

IN JUST TWENTY YEARS, THE DREAM HAD COME MORE THAN TRUE. ELVIS PRESLEY, ACKNOWLEDGED KING OF SHOW-BUSINESS, MADE A FILM CALLED 'CHARRO'...

THE FANS LOVED HIS ROUGH, TOUGH WESTERN STYLE...

BUT THE FILM WAS ONE OF A LONG LINE OF REAL SECOND-RATERS. THE KING, A VIRTUAL RECLUSE, HAD CHURNED OUT WHAT THE CRITICS HAD TERMED 'MILES OF RUBBISH'...

APART FROM 'HARUM SCARUM' THERE WAS 'SPIN OUT'...

...'KISSIN' COUSINS'...

...'FRANKIE AND JOHNNY'...

HE EVEN APPEARED IN SCUBA GEAR IN 'EASY COME, EASY GO'...

THEN, AT LAST, ELVIS THREW OFF THE DEJECTION THAT HAD KEPT HIM PENNED FOR EIGHT LONG YEARS. HE HAD A WIFE, PRISCILLA, AND A DAUGHTER, LISA MARIE. MAYBE IT WAS THAT, THAT SNAPPED HIM OUT OF IT...

I'M GONNA MAKE A TELEVISION SPECIAL, HONEY. LIVE AUDIENCE, AND ALL. IT'S TIME I MADE MY COME-BACK...

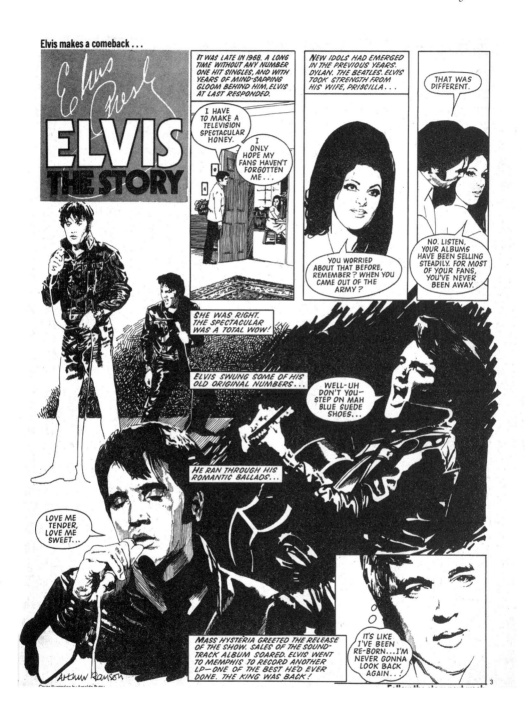

181

BOTH FOR ELVIS AND HIS FANS, THE MIDDLE 1970s WERE HARROWING, SAD YEARS. NONE BUT HIS CLOSEST ASSOCIATES KNEW IT AT THE TIME, BUT HE WAS REGULARLY IN AND OUT OF MEMPHIS BAPTIST HOSPITAL...

I DON'T KNOW WHAT'S DOING IT. THE BREAK-UP OF HIS MARRIAGE? THE PRESSURE OF BEING THE WORLD'S GREATEST STAR..?

THE AWFUL THING IS, HE DOESN'T SEEM TO CARE!

THE FANS? THEY GUESSED THE WORST FROM HIS PERFORMANCES. SOMETIMES, HE'D FORGET THE WORDS OF A SONG...

HE'S JUST STOPPED. WHAT'S THE MATTER WITH HIM..?

HE LOOKS— EXHAUSTED...

BETWEEN SETS, HE WOULD OFTEN HAVE TO SIT IN A CHAIR...

IN A LUCID MOMENT, HE ONCE CONFIDED IN HIS FRIEND, PAT BOONE.

I AIN'T NEVER GONNA LIVE TO BE AN OLD MAN. MY MOMMA WENT YOUNG, AN' I'M LIKE HER. GO LIKE HER...

DON'T TALK THAT WAY, ELVIS...

THERE WERE TIMES THOUGH, DESPITE THE INCREASING SCORN OF THE CRITICS, THAT ELVIS COULD REALLY WOW HIS AUDIENCE...

IN PRIVATE, HE BEGAN TO FLY INTO TERRIBLE, PASSIONATE RAGES. EXPLODING IN ANGER AT THE SLIGHTEST OF REASONS...

A COUPLE OF TIMES, HE EVEN COLLAPSED ON STAGE...

OH, NO! NO!

183

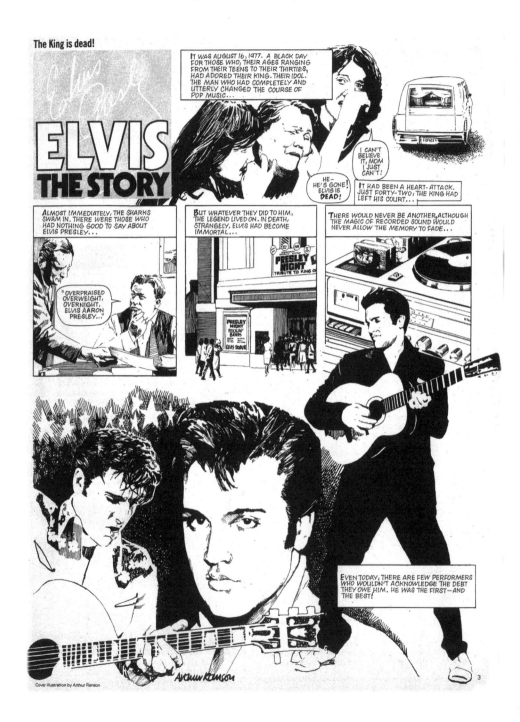

Elvis loved comic books and when he was younger his favorite comic book was Captain Marvel Jr.

Elvis was fascinated with Captain Marvel Jr., "The Mightiest
Boy in the World."

Many people now feel that Elvis modeled himself after Captain Marvel Jr., and even looked and dressed like the superhero.

Elvis fans have noticed that Elvis apparently took on a superhero persona, dressing in a cape, large belt and acting like his boyhood hero Captain Marvel Jr.

Elvis even used the lightning bolt symbol on Captain Marvel Jr.'s chest as his personal gift necklace which he gave to his staff with the letters "T, C, B" which meant "Taking of Business."

ANCIENT ALIENS ON THE MOON
By Mike Bara
What did NASA find in their explorations of the solar system that they may have kept from the general public? How ancient really are these ruins on the Moon? Using official NASA and Russian photos of the Moon, Bara looks at vast cityscapes and domes in the Sinus Medii region as well as glass domes in the Crisium region. Bara also takes a detailed look at the mission of Apollo 17 and the case that this was a salvage mission, primarily concerned with investigating an opening into a massive hexagonal ruin near the landing site. Chapters include: The History of Lunar Anomalies; The Early 20th Century; Sinus Medii; To the Moon Alice!; Mare Crisium; Yes, Virginia, We Really Went to the Moon; Apollo 17; more. Tons of photos of the Moon examined for possible structures and other anomalies.
240 Pages. 6x9 Paperback. Illustrated.. $19.95. Code: AAOM

ANCIENT TECHNOLOGY IN PERU & BOLIVIA
By David Hatcher Childress
Childress speculates on the existence of a sunken city in Lake Titicaca and reveals new evidence that the Sumerians may have arrived in South America 4,000 years ago. He demonstrates that the use of "keystone cuts" with metal clamps poured into them to secure megalithic construction was an advanced technology used all over the world, from the Andes to Egypt, Greece and Southeast Asia. He maintains that only power tools could have made the intricate articulation and drill holes found in extremely hard granite and basalt blocks in Bolivia and Peru, and that the megalith builders had to have had advanced methods for moving and stacking gigantic blocks of stone, some weighing over 100 tons.
340 Pages. 6x9 Paperback. Illustrated.. $19.95 Code: ATP

THE ILLUSTRATED DOOM SURVIVAL GUIDE
Don't Panic!
By Matt "DoomGuy" Victor
With over 500 very detailed and easy-to-understand illustrations, this book literally shows you how to do things like build a fire with whatever is at hand, perform field surgeries, identify and test foodstuffs, and form twine, snares and fishhooks. In any doomsday scenario, being able to provide things of real value—such as clothing, tools, medical supplies, labor, food and water—will be of the utmost importance. This book gives you the particulars to help you survive in any environment with little to no equipment, and make it through the first critical junctures after a disaster. Beyond any disaster you will have the knowledge to rebuild shelter, farm from seed to seed, raise animals, treat medical problems, predict the weather and protect your loved ones.
356 Pages. 6x9 Paperback. Illustrated. $20.00. Code: IDSG

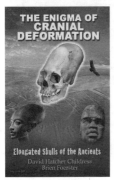

THE ENIGMA OF CRANIAL DEFORMATION
Elongated Skulls of the Ancients
By David Hatcher Childress and Brien Foerster
In a book filled with over a hundred astonishing photos and a color photo section, Childress and Foerster take us to Peru, Bolivia, Egypt, Malta, China, Mexico and other places in search of strange elongated skulls and other cranial deformation. The puzzle of why diverse ancient people—even on remote Pacific Islands—would use head-binding to create elongated heads is mystifying. Where did they even get this idea? Did some people naturally look this way—with long narrow heads? Were they some alien race? Were they an elite race that roamed the entire planet? Why do anthropologists rarely talk about cranial deformation and know so little about it?
250 Pages. 6x9 Paperback. Illustrated. $19.95. Code: ECD

LOST CITIES & ANCIENT MYSTERIES OF THE SOUTHWEST
By David Hatcher Childress

Join David as he starts in northern Mexico and searches for the lost mines of the Aztecs. He continues north to west Texas, delving into the mysteries of Big Bend, including mysterious Phoenician tablets discovered there and the strange lights of Marfa. Then into New Mexico where he stumbles upon a hollow mountain with a billion dollars of gold bars hidden deep inside it! In Arizona he investigates tales of Egyptian catacombs in the Grand Canyon, cruises along the Devil's Highway, and tackles the century-old mystery of the Lost Dutchman mine. In Nevada and California Childress checks out the rumors of mummified giants and weird tunnels in Death Valley, plus he searches the Mohave Desert for the mysterious remains of ancient dwellers alongside lakes that dried up tens of thousands of years ago. It's a full-tilt blast down the back roads of the Southwest in search of the weird and wondrous mysteries of the past!

486 Pages. 6x9 Paperback. Illustrated. Bibliography. $19.95. Code: LCSW

TECHNOLOGY OF THE GODS
The Incredible Sciences of the Ancients
by David Hatcher Childress

Childress looks at the technology that was allegedly used in Atlantis and the theory that the Great Pyramid of Egypt was originally a gigantic power station. He examines tales of ancient flight and the technology that it involved; how the ancients used electricity; megalithic building techniques; the use of crystal lenses and the fire from the gods; evidence of various high tech weapons in the past, including atomic weapons; ancient metallurgy and heavy machinery; the role of modern inventors such as Nikola Tesla in bringing ancient technology back into modern use; impossible artifacts; and more.

356 PAGES. 6x9 PAPERBACK. ILLUSTRATED. BIBLIOGRAPHY. $16.95. CODE: TGOD

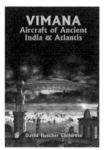

VIMANA AIRCRAFT OF ANCIENT INDIA & ATLANTIS
by David Hatcher Childress, introduction by Ivan T. Sanderson

In this incredible volume on ancient India, authentic Indian texts such as the *Ramayana* and the *Mahabharata* are used to prove that ancient aircraft were in use more than four thousand years ago. Included in this book is the entire Fourth Century BC manuscript *Vimaanika Shastra* by the ancient author Maharishi Bharadwaaja. Also included are chapters on Atlantean technology, the incredible Rama Empire of India and the devastating wars that destroyed it.

334 PAGES. 6x9 PAPERBACK. ILLUSTRATED. $15.95. CODE: VAA

LOST CONTINENTS & THE HOLLOW EARTH
I Remember Lemuria and the Shaver Mystery
by David Hatcher Childress & Richard Shaver

Shaver's rare 1948 book *I Remember Lemuria* is reprinted in its entirety, and the book is packed with illustrations from Ray Palmer's *Amazing Stories* magazine of the 1940s. Palmer and Shaver told of tunnels running through the earth—tunnels inhabited by the Deros and Teros, humanoids from an ancient spacefaring race that had inhabited the earth, eventually going underground, hundreds of thousands of years ago. Childress discusses the famous hollow earth books and delves deep into whatever reality may be behind the stories of tunnels in the earth. Operation High Jump to Antarctica in 1947 and Admiral Byrd's bizarre statements, tunnel systems in South America and Tibet, the underground world of Agartha, the belief of UFOs coming from the South Pole, more.

344 PAGES. 6x9 PAPERBACK. ILLUSTRATED. $16.95. CODE: LCHE

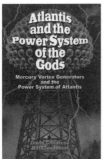

ATLANTIS & THE POWER SYSTEM OF THE GODS
by David Hatcher Childress and Bill Clendenon
Childress' fascinating analysis of Nikola Tesla's broadcast system in light of Edgar Cayce's "Terrible Crystal" and the obelisks of ancient Egypt and Ethiopia. Includes: Atlantis and its crystal power towers that broadcast energy; how these incredible power stations may still exist today; inventor Nikola Tesla's nearly identical system of power transmission; Mercury Proton Gyros and mercury vortex propulsion; more. Richly illustrated, and packed with evidence that Atlantis not only existed—it had a world-wide energy system more sophisticated than ours today.
246 PAGES. 6x9 PAPERBACK. ILLUSTRATED. $15.95. CODE: APSG

THE ANTI-GRAVITY HANDBOOK
edited by David Hatcher Childress
The new expanded compilation of material on Anti-Gravity, Free Energy, Flying Saucer Propulsion, UFOs, Suppressed Technology, NASA Cover-ups and more. Highly illustrated with patents, technical illustrations and photos. This revised and expanded edition has more material, including photos of Area 51, Nevada, the government's secret testing facility. This classic on weird science is back in a new format!
230 PAGES. 7x10 PAPERBACK. ILLUSTRATED. $16.95. CODE: AGH

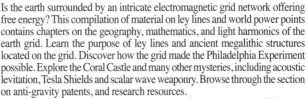

ANTI-GRAVITY & THE WORLD GRID
Is the earth surrounded by an intricate electromagnetic grid network offering free energy? This compilation of material on ley lines and world power points contains chapters on the geography, mathematics, and light harmonics of the earth grid. Learn the purpose of ley lines and ancient megalithic structures located on the grid. Discover how the grid made the Philadelphia Experiment possible. Explore the Coral Castle and many other mysteries, including acoustic levitation, Tesla Shields and scalar wave weaponry. Browse through the section on anti-gravity patents, and research resources.
274 PAGES. 7x10 PAPERBACK. ILLUSTRATED. $14.95. CODE: AGW

ANTI-GRAVITY & THE UNIFIED FIELD
edited by David Hatcher Childress
Is Einstein's Unified Field Theory the answer to all of our energy problems? Explored in this compilation of material is how gravity, electricity and magnetism manifest from a unified field around us. Why artificial gravity is possible; secrets of UFO propulsion; free energy; Nikola Tesla and anti-gravity airships of the 20s and 30s; flying saucers as superconducting whirls of plasma; anti-mass generators; vortex propulsion; suppressed technology; government cover-ups; gravitational pulse drive; spacecraft & more.
240 PAGES. 7x10 PAPERBACK. ILLUSTRATED. $14.95. CODE: AGU

THE TIME TRAVEL HANDBOOK
A Manual of Practical Teleportation & Time Travel
edited by David Hatcher Childress
The Time Travel Handbook takes the reader beyond the government experiments and deep into the uncharted territory of early time travellers such as Nikola Tesla and Guglielmo Marconi and their alleged time travel experiments, as well as the Wilson Brothers of EMI and their connection to the Philadelphia Experiment—the U.S. Navy's forays into invisibility, time travel, and teleportation. Childress looks into the claims of time travelling individuals, and investigates the unusual claim that the pyramids on Mars were built in the future and sent back in time. A highly visual, large format book, with patents, photos and schematics. Be the first on your block to build your own time travel device!
316 PAGES. 7x10 PAPERBACK. ILLUSTRATED. $16.95. CODE: TTH

MAPS OF THE ANCIENT SEA KINGS
Evidence of Advanced Civilization in the Ice Age
by Charles H. Hapgood
Charles Hapgood has found the evidence in the Piri Reis Map that shows Antarctica, the Hadji Ahmed map, the Oronteus Finaeus and other amazing maps. Hapgood concluded that these maps were made from more ancient maps from the various ancient archives around the world, now lost. Not only were these unknown people more advanced in mapmaking than any people prior to the 18th century, it appears they mapped all the continents. The Americas were mapped thousands of years before Columbus. Antarctica was mapped when its coasts were free of ice!

316 PAGES. 7x10 PAPERBACK. ILLUSTRATED. BIBLIOGRAPHY & INDEX. $19.95. CODE: MASK

PATH OF THE POLE
Cataclysmic Pole Shift Geology
by Charles H. Hapgood
Maps of the Ancient Sea Kings author Hapgood's classic book *Path of the Pole* is back in print! Hapgood researched Antarctica, ancient maps and the geological record to conclude that the Earth's crust has slipped on the inner core many times in the past, changing the position of the pole. *Path of the Pole* discusses the various "pole shifts" in Earth's past, giving evidence for each one, and moves on to possible future pole shifts.

356 PAGES. 6x9 PAPERBACK. ILLUSTRATED. $16.95. CODE: POP

SECRETS OF THE HOLY LANCE
The Spear of Destiny in History & Legend
by Jerry E. Smith
Secrets of the Holy Lance traces the Spear from its possession by Constantine, Rome's first Christian Caesar, to Charlemagne's claim that with it he ruled the Holy Roman Empire by Divine Right, and on through two thousand years of kings and emperors, until it came within Hitler's grasp—and beyond! Did it rest for a while in Antarctic ice? Is it now hidden in Europe, awaiting the next person to claim its awesome power? Neither debunking nor worshiping, *Secrets of the Holy Lance* seeks to pierce the veil of myth and mystery around the Spear. Mere belief that it was infused with magic by virtue of its shedding the Savior's blood has made men kings. But what if it's more? What are "the powers it serves"?

312 PAGES. 6x9 PAPERBACK. ILLUSTRATED. BIBLIOGRAPHY. $16.95. CODE: SOHL

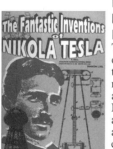

THE FANTASTIC INVENTIONS OF NIKOLA TESLA
by Nikola Tesla with additional material by
David Hatcher Childress
This book is a readable compendium of patents, diagrams, photos and explanations of the many incredible inventions of the originator of the modern era of electrification. In Tesla's own words are such topics as wireless transmission of power, death rays, and radio-controlled airships. In addition, rare material on a secret city built at a remote jungle site in South America by one of Tesla's students, Guglielmo Marconi. Marconi's secret group claims to have built flying saucers in the 1940s and to have gone to Mars in the early 1950s! Incredible photos of these Tesla craft are included. •His plan to transmit free electricity into the atmosphere. •How electrical devices would work using only small antennas. •Why unlimited power could be utilized anywhere on earth. •How radio and radar technology can be used as death-ray weapons in Star Wars.

342 PAGES. 6x9 PAPERBACK. ILLUSTRATED. $16.95. CODE: FINT

REICH OF THE BLACK SUN
Nazi Secret Weapons & the Cold War Allied Legend
by Joseph P. Farrell

Why were the Allies worried about an atom bomb attack by the Germans in 1944? Why did the Soviets threaten to use poison gas against the Germans? Why did Hitler in 1945 insist that holding Prague could win the war for the Third Reich? Why did US General George Patton's Third Army race for the Skoda works at Pilsen in Czechoslovakia instead of Berlin? Why did the US Army not test the uranium atom bomb it dropped on Hiroshima? Why did the Luftwaffe fly a non-stop round trip mission to within twenty miles of New York City in 1944? *Reich of the Black Sun* takes the reader on a scientific-historical journey in order to answer these questions. Arguing that Nazi Germany actually won the race for the atom bomb in late 1944, **352 PAGES. 6x9 PAPERBACK. ILLUSTRATED. BIBLIOGRAPHY. $16.95.** CODE: **ROBS**

THE GIZA DEATH STAR
The Paleophysics of the Great Pyramid & the Military Complex at Giza
by Joseph P. Farrell

Was the Giza complex part of a military installation over 10,000 years ago? Chapters include: An Archaeology of Mass Destruction, Thoth and Theories; The Machine Hypothesis; Pythagoras, Plato, Planck, and the Pyramid; The Weapon Hypothesis; Encoded Harmonics of the Planck Units in the Great Pyramid; High Frequency Direct Current "Impulse" Technology; The Grand Gallery and its Crystals: Gravito-acoustic Resonators; The Other Two Large Pyramids; the "Causeways," and the "Temples"; A Phase Conjugate Howitzer; Evidence of the Use of Weapons of Mass Destruction in Ancient Times; more.
290 PAGES. 6x9 PAPERBACK. ILLUSTRATED. $16.95. CODE: **GDS**

THE GIZA DEATH STAR DEPLOYED
The Physics & Engineering of the Great Pyramid
by Joseph P. Farrell

Farrell expands on his thesis that the Great Pyramid was a maser, designed as a weapon and eventually deployed—with disastrous results to the solar system. Includes: Exploding Planets: A Brief History of the Exoteric and Esoteric Investigations of the Great Pyramid; No Machines, Please!; The Stargate Conspiracy; The Scalar Weapons; Message or Machine?; A Tesla Analysis of the Putative Physics and Engineering of the Giza Death Star; Cohering the Zero Point, Vacuum Energy, Flux: Feedback Loops and Tetrahedral Physics; and more.
290 PAGES. 6x9 PAPERBACK. ILLUSTRATED. $16.95. CODE: **GDSD**

THE GIZA DEATH STAR DESTROYED
The Ancient War For Future Science
by Joseph P. Farrell

Farrell moves on to events of the final days of the Giza Death Star and its awesome power. These final events, eventually leading up to the destruction of this giant machine, are dissected one by one, leading us to the eventual abandonment of the Giza Military Complex—an event that hurled civilization back into the Stone Age. Chapters include: The Mars-Earth Connection; The Lost "Root Races" and the Moral Reasons for the Flood; The Destruction of Krypton: The Electrodynamic Solar System, Exploding Planets and Ancient Wars; Turning the Stream of the Flood: the Origin of Secret Societies and Esoteric Traditions; The Quest to Recover Ancient Mega-Technology; Non-Equilibrium Paleophysics; Monatomic Paleophysics; Frequencies, Vortices and Mass Particles; "Acoustic" Intensity of Fields; The Pyramid of Crystals; tons more.
292 pages. 6x9 paperback. Illustrated. $16.95. Code: GDES

ROSWELL AND THE REICH
The Nazi Connection
By Joseph P. Farrell
Farrell has meticulously reviewed the best-known Roswell research from UFO-ET advocates and skeptics alike, as well as some little-known source material, and comes to a radically different scenario of what happened in Roswell, New Mexico in July 1947, and why the US military has continued to cover it up to this day. Farrell presents a fascinating case sure to disturb both ET believers and disbelievers, namely, that what crashed may have been representative of an independent postwar Nazi power—an extraterritorial Reich monitoring its old enemy, America, and the continuing development of the very technologies confiscated from Germany at the end of the War.
540 pages. 6x9 Paperback. Illustrated. $19.95. Code: RWR

SECRETS OF THE UNIFIED FIELD
The Philadelphia Experiment, the Nazi Bell, and the Discarded Theory
by Joseph P. Farrell
Farrell examines the now discarded Unified Field Theory. American and German wartime scientists and engineers determined that, while the theory was incomplete, it could nevertheless be engineered. Chapters include: The Meanings of "Torsion"; Wringing an Aluminum Can; The Mistake in Unified Field Theories and Their Discarding by Contemporary Physics; Three Routes to the Doomsday Weapon: Quantum Potential, Torsion, and Vortices; Tesla's Meeting with FDR; Arnold Sommerfeld and Electromagnetic Radar Stealth; Electromagnetic Phase Conjugations, Phase Conjugate Mirrors, and Templates; The Unified Field Theory, the Torsion Tensor, and Igor Witkowski's Idea of the Plasma Focus; tons more.
340 pages. 6x9 Paperback. Illustrated. $18.95. Code: SOUF

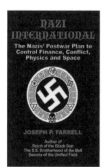

NAZI INTERNATIONAL
The Nazi's Postwar Plan to Control Finance, Conflict, Physics and Space
by Joseph P. Farrell
Beginning with prewar corporate partnerships in the USA, including some with the Bush family, he moves on to the surrender of Nazi Germany, and evacuation plans of the Germans. He then covers the vast, and still-little-known recreation of Nazi Germany in South America with help of Juan Peron, I.G. Farben and Martin Bormann. Farrell then covers Nazi Germany's penetration of the Muslim world including Wilhelm Voss and Otto Skorzeny in Gamel Abdul Nasser's Egypt before moving on to the development and control of new energy technologies including the Bariloche Fusion Project, Dr. Philo Farnsworth's Plasmator, and the work of Dr. Nikolai Kozyrev. Finally, Farrell discusses the Nazi desire to control space, and examines their connection with NASA, the esoteric meaning of NASA Mission Patches.
412 pages. 6x9 Paperback. Illustrated. $19.95. Code: NZIN

ARKTOS
The Polar Myth in Science, Symbolism & Nazi Survival
by Joscelyn Godwin
Explored are the many tales of an ancient race said to have lived in the Arctic regions, such as Thule and Hyperborea. Progressing onward, he looks at modern polar legends: including the survival of Hitler, German bases in Antarctica, UFOs, the hollow earth, and the hidden kingdoms of Agartha and Shambala. Chapters include: Prologue in Hyperborea; The Golden Age; The Northern Lights; The Arctic Homeland; The Aryan Myth; The Thule Society; The Black Order; The Hidden Lands; Agartha and the Polaires; Shambhala; The Hole at the Pole; Antarctica; more.
220 Pages. 6x9 Paperback. Illustrated. Bib. Index. $16.95. Code: ARK

COVERT WARS AND BREAKAWAY CIVILIZATIONS
By Joseph P. Farrell
Farrell delves into the creation of breakaway civilizations by the Nazis in South America and other parts of the world. He discusses the advanced technology that they took with them at the end of the war and the psychological war that they waged for decades on America and NATO. He investigates the secret space programs currently sponsored by the breakaway civilizations and the current militaries in control of planet Earth. Plenty of astounding accounts, documents and speculation on the incredible alternative history of hidden conflicts and secret space programs that began when World War II officially "ended."
292 Pages. 6x9 Paperback. Illustrated. $19.95. Code: BCCW

PRODIGAL GENIUS
The Life of Nikola Tesla
by John J. O'Neill
This special edition of O'Neill's book has many rare photographs of Tesla and his most advanced inventions. Tesla's eccentric personality gives his life story a strange romantic quality. He made his first million before he was forty, yet gave up his royalties in a gesture of friendship, and died almost in poverty. Tesla could see an invention in 3-D, from every angle, within his mind, before it was built; how he refused to accept the Nobel Prize; his friendships with Mark Twain, George Westinghouse and competition with Thomas Edison. Tesla is revealed as a figure of genius whose influence on the world reaches into the far future. Deluxe, illustrated edition.
408 pages. 6x9 Paperback. Illustrated. Bibliography. $18.95. Code: PRG

HAARP
The Ultimate Weapon of the Conspiracy
by Jerry Smith
The HAARP project in Alaska is one of the most controversial projects ever undertaken by the U.S. Government. At at worst, HAARP could be the most dangerous device ever created, a futuristic technology that is everything from super-beam weapon to world-wide mind control device. Topics include Over-the-Horizon Radar and HAARP, Mind Control, ELF and HAARP, The Telsa Connection, The Russian Woodpecker, GWEN & HAARP, Earth Penetrating Tomography, Weather Modification, Secret Science of the Conspiracy, more. Includes the complete 1987 Eastlund patent for his pulsed super-weapon that he claims was stolen by the HAARP Project.
256 pages. 6x9 Paperback. Illustrated. Bib. $14.95. Code: HARP

WEATHER WARFARE
The Military's Plan to Draft Mother Nature
by Jerry E. Smith
Weather modification in the form of cloud seeding to increase snow packs in the Sierras or suppress hail over Kansas is now an everyday affair. Underground nuclear tests in Nevada have set off earthquakes. A Russian company has been offering to sell typhoons (hurricanes) on demand since the 1990s. Scientists have been searching for ways to move hurricanes for over fifty years. In the same amount of time we went from the Wright Brothers to Neil Armstrong. Hundreds of environmental and weather modifying technologies have been patented in the United States alone – and hundreds more are being developed in civilian, academic, military and quasi-military laboratories around the world *at this moment!* Numerous ongoing military programs do inject aerosols at high altitude for communications and surveillance operations.
304 Pages. 6x9 Paperback. Illustrated. Bib. $18.95. Code: WWAR

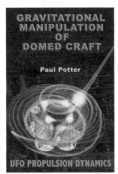

GRAVITATIONAL MANIPULATION OF DOMED CRAFT
UFO Propulsion Dynamics
by Paul E. Potter

Potter's precise and lavish illustrations allow the reader to enter directly into the realm of the advanced technological engineer and to understand, quite straightforwardly, the aliens' methods of energy manipulation: their methods of electrical power generation; how they purposely designed their craft to employ the kinds of energy dynamics that are exclusive to space (discoverable in our astrophysics) in order that their craft may generate both attractive and repulsive gravitational forces; their control over the mass-density matrix surrounding their craft enabling them to alter their physical dimensions and even manufacture their own frame of reference in respect to time. Includes a 16-page color insert.

624 pages. 7x10 Paperback. Illustrated. References. $24.00. Code: GMDC

TAPPING THE ZERO POINT ENERGY
Free Energy & Anti-Gravity in Today's Physics
by Moray B. King

King explains how free energy and anti-gravity are possible. The theories of the zero point energy maintain there are tremendous fluctuations of electrical field energy imbedded within the fabric of space. This book tells how, in the 1930s, inventor T. Henry Moray could produce a fifty kilowatt "free energy" machine; how an electrified plasma vortex creates anti-gravity; how the Pons/Fleischmann "cold fusion" experiment could produce tremendous heat without fusion; and how certain experiments might produce a gravitational anomaly.

180 PAGES. 5x8 PAPERBACK. ILLUSTRATED. $12.95. CODE: TAP

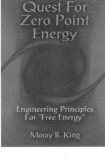

QUEST FOR ZERO-POINT ENERGY
Engineering Principles for "Free Energy"
by Moray B. King

King expands, with diagrams, on how free energy and anti-gravity are possible. The theories of zero point energy maintain there are tremendous fluctuations of electrical field energy embedded within the fabric of space. King explains the following topics: TFundamentals of a Zero-Point Energy Technology; Vacuum Energy Vortices; The Super Tube; Charge Clusters: The Basis of Zero-Point Energy Inventions; Vortex Filaments, Torsion Fields and the Zero-Point Energy; Transforming the Planet with a Zero-Point Energy Experiment; Dual Vortex Forms: The Key to a Large Zero-Point Energy Coherence. Packed with diagrams, patents and photos.

224 PAGES. 6x9 PAPERBACK. ILLUSTRATED. $14.95. CODE: QZPE

DARK MOON
Apollo and the Whistleblowers
by Mary Bennett and David Percy

Did you know a second craft was going to the Moon at the same time as Apollo 11? Do you know that potentially lethal radiation is prevalent throughout deep space? Do you know there are serious discrepancies in the account of the Apollo 13 'accident'? Did you know that 'live' color TV from the Moon was not actually live at all? Did you know that the Lunar Surface Camera had no viewfinder? Do you know that lighting was used in the Apollo photographs—yet no lighting equipment was taken to the Moon? All these questions, and more, are discussed in great detail by British researchers Bennett and Percy in *Dark Moon*, the definitive book (nearly 600 pages) on the possible faking of the Apollo Moon missions. Tons of NASA photos analyzed for possible deceptions.

568 PAGES. 6x9 PAPERBACK. ILLUSTRATED. BIBLIOGRAPHY. INDEX. $32.00. CODE: DMO

SECRETS OF THE UNIFIED FIELD
The Philadelphia Experiment, the Nazi Bell, and the Discarded Theory
by Joseph P. Farrell

Farrell examines the now discarded Unified Field Theory. American and German wartime scientists and engineers determined that, while the theory was incomplete, it could nevertheless be engineered. Chapters include: The Meanings of "Torsion"; Wringing an Aluminum Can; The Mistake in Unified Field Theories and Their Discarding by Contemporary Physics; Three Routes to the Doomsday Weapon: Quantum Potential, Torsion, and Vortices; Tesla's Meeting with FDR; Arnold Sommerfeld and Electromagnetic Radar Stealth; Electromagnetic Phase Conjugations, Phase Conjugate Mirrors, and Templates; The Unified Field Theory, the Torsion Tensor, and Witkowski's Idea of the Plasma Focus; tons more.

340 pages. 6x9 Paperback. Illustrated. $18.95. Code: SOUF

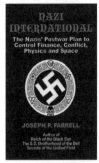

NAZI INTERNATIONAL
The Nazi's Postwar Plan to Control Finance, Conflict, Physics and Space
by Joseph P. Farrell

Beginning with prewar corporate partnerships in the USA, including some with the Bush family, he moves on to the surrender of Nazi Germany, and evacuation plans of the Germans. He then covers the vast, and still-little-known recreation of Nazi Germany in South America with help of Juan Peron, I.G. Farben and Martin Bormann. Farrell then covers he development and control of new energy technologies including the Bariloche Fusion Project, Dr. Philo Farnsworth's Plasmator, and the work of Dr. Nikolai Kozyrev. Finally, Farrell discusses the Nazi desire to control space, and examines their connection with NASA, the esoteric meaning of NASA Mission Patches.

412 pages. 6x9 Paperback. Illustrated. $19.95. Code: NZIN

SAUCERS, SWASTIKAS AND PSYOPS
By Joseph P. Farrell

Farrell discusses SS Commando Otto Skorzeny; George Adamski; the alleged Hannebu and Vril craft of the Third Reich; The Strange Case of Dr. Hermann Oberth; Nazis in the US and their connections to "UFO contactees." Chapters include: The Nov. 20, 1952 Contact: The Memes are Implants; George Hunt Williamson and the Baileys; William Pelley and the American Fascists; The Messages from "ET"; The Venusian and "The Bomb"; Adamski's ETs and Religion: The Interplanetary Federation of Brotherhood and the "Übermensch ET"; Adamski's Technological Descriptions and Another ET Message: The Danger of Weaponized Gravity; Adamski's Retro-Looking Saucers, and the Nazi Saucer Myth; more.

262 Pages. 6x9 Paperback. Illustrated. $19.95. Code: SSPY

PARAPOLITICS!
Conspiracy in Contemporary America
by Kenn Thomas

From the Kennedy assassination to 9/11, Thomas examines the underlying parapolitics that animate the secret elites and the war-ravaged planet they manipulate. Contents include: Octopus Redux; Previously unpublished interview with the girlfriend of Octopus investigator Danny Casolaro; Orgone; Wilhelm Reich: Eisenhower's secret ally against the aliens; Clinton era conspiracies; You Too Can Be a Researcher: How to use the Freedom of Information Act; Anthrax Terrorists; Media Mindwash; 9/11 Commission Omission, and much, much more.

340 Pages. 6x9 Paperback. Illustrated. $20.00. Code: PPOL

LIQUID CONSPIRACY
JFK, LSD, the CIA, Area 51 & UFOs
by George Piccard
Underground author George Piccard on the politics of LSD, mind control, and Kennedy's involvement with Area 51 and UFOs. Reveals JFK's LSD experiences with Mary Pinchot-Meyer. The plot thickens with an ever expanding web of CIA involvement, from underground bases with UFOs seen by JFK and Marilyn Monroe (among others) to a vaster conspiracy that affects every government agency from NASA to the Justice Department. This may have been the reason that Marilyn Monroe and actress-columnist Dorothy Kilgallen were both murdered. Focusing on the bizarre side of history, *Liquid Conspiracy* takes the reader on a psychedelic tour de force. This is your government on drugs!
264 Pages. 6x9 Paperback. Illustrated. $14.95. Code: LIQC

MIND CONTROL, OSWALD & JFK
Introduction by Kenn Thomas
In 1969 the strange book *Were We Controlled?* was published which maintained that Lee Harvey Oswald was a special agent who was also a Mind Control subject who had received an implant in 1960 at a Russian hospital. Thomas examines the evidence that Oswald had been an early recipient of the Mind Control implant technology and this startling role in the Kennedy Assassination. Also: the RHIC-EDOM Mind Control aspects concerning the RFK assassination and details the history of implant technology.
256 Pages. 6x9 Paperback. Illustrated. References. $16.00. Code: MCOJ

MIND CONTROL, WORLD CONTROL
The Encyclopedia of Mind Control
by Jim Keith
Keith uncovers a surprising amount of information on the technology, experimentation and implementation of Mind Control technology. Various chapters in this shocking book are on early C.I.A. experiments such as Project Artichoke and Project RIC-EDOM, the methodology and technology of implants, Mind Control Assassins and Couriers, various famous "Mind Control" victims such as Sirhan Sirhan and Candy Jones. Also featured in this book are chapters on how Mind Control technology may be linked to some UFO activity and "UFO abductions.
256 Pages. 6x9 Paperback. Illustrated. References. $14.95. Code: MCWC

MASS CONTROL
Engineering Human Consciousness
by Jim Keith
Conspiracy expert Keith's final book on mind control, Project Monarch, and mass manipulation presents chilling evidence that we are indeed spinning a Matrix. Keith describes the New Man, where conception of reality is a dance of electronic images fired into his forebrain, a gossamer construction of his masters, designed so that he will not perceive the actual. His happiness is delivered to him through a tube or an electronic connection. His God lurks behind an electronic curtain; when the curtain is pulled away we find the CIA sorcerer, the media manipulator... Chapters on the CIA, Tavistock, Jolly West and the Violence Center, Guerrilla Mindwar, Brice Taylor, other recent "victims," more.
256 Pages. 6x9 Paperback. Illustrated. Index. $16.95. code: MASC

ORDER FORM

10% Discount When You Order 3 or More Items!

One Adventure Place
P.O. Box 74
Kempton, Illinois 60946
United States of America
Tel.: 815-253-6390 • Fax: 815-253-6300
Email: auphq@frontiernet.net
http://www.adventuresunlimitedpress.com

ORDERING INSTRUCTIONS

✓ Remit by USD$ Check, Money Order or Credit Card

✓ Visa, Master Card, Discover & AmEx Accepted

✓ Paypal Payments Can Be Made To:

  info@wexclub.com

✓ Prices May Change Without Notice

✓ 10% Discount for 3 or More Items

SHIPPING CHARGES

United States

✓ Postal Book Rate { $4.50 First Item / 50¢ Each Additional Item

✓ POSTAL BOOK RATE Cannot Be Tracked!
  Not responsible for non-delivery.

✓ Priority Mail { $6.00 First Item / $2.00 Each Additional Item

✓ UPS { $7.00 First Item / $1.50 Each Additional Item

  NOTE: UPS Delivery Available to Mainland USA Only

Canada

✓ Postal Air Mail { $15.00 First Item / $3.00 Each Additional Item

✓ Personal Checks or Bank Drafts MUST BE US$ and Drawn on a US Bank

✓ Canadian Postal Money Orders OK

✓ Payment MUST BE US$

All Other Countries

✓ Sorry, No Surface Delivery!

✓ Postal Air Mail { $19.00 First Item / $7.00 Each Additional Item

✓ Checks and Money Orders MUST BE US$ and Drawn on a US Bank or branch.

✓ Paypal Payments Can Be Made in US$ To:
  info@wexclub.com

SPECIAL NOTES

✓ RETAILERS: Standard Discounts Available

✓ BACKORDERS: We Backorder all Out-of-Stock Items Unless Otherwise Requested

✓ PRO FORMA INVOICES: Available on Request

✓ DVD Return Policy: Replace defective DVDs only

ORDER ONLINE AT: www.adventuresunlimitedpress.com

10% Discount When You Order 3 or More Items!

Please check: ☑

☐ This is my first order   ☐ I have ordered before

Name

Address

City

State/Province _____ Postal Code

Country

Phone: Day _____ Evening

Fax _____ Email

Item Code	Item Description	Qty	Total

Please check: ☑

	Subtotal ▶	
	Less Discount-10% for 3 or more items ▶	
☐ Postal-Surface	Balance ▶	
☐ Postal-Air Mail (Priority in USA)	Illinois Residents 6.25% Sales Tax ▶	
	Previous Credit ▶	
☐ UPS	Shipping ▶	
(Mainland USA only)	Total (check/MO in USD$ only) ▶	
☐ Visa/MasterCard/Discover/American Express		

Card Number:

Expiration Date: _____ Security Code:

✓ SEND A CATALOG TO A FRIEND: